25285

D0197821

Library
Oakland S.U.M.

Dear Reader,

This book is intended to serve as a brief and cursory introduction to the great religion of Islam. It is not intended to be an exhaustive, authoritative, or academic treatise or dissertation. This book is written in the form of question and answer format. The author has compiled, over a period of twenty-five years, the most frequently asked questions about Islam which he has received during lectures and presentations to numerous audiences world-wide. The question will be stated first, and the answer will follow.

For those interested in a further study of Islam, please note the Suggested Reading List at the close of this book. Also, a brief Glossary of Terms is included as a quick reference for the reader.

May God grant you an open mind and heart as you read and learn the basic teachings and truths of Islam, and the Common Ground that exists between Islam and Christianity.

William W. Baker, Author

MORE IN COMMON THAN YOU THINK

THE BRIDGE BETWEEN ISLAM AND CHRISTIANITY

By William W. Baker

© 1998. All Rights Reserved.

No part of this book may be reproduced, translated, stored in a retrieval system, or transmitted, in any form by any means, electronic, mechanical, photo-copying, recording, or otherwise, without prior written permission of the author.

Unless otherwise noted, Scripture quotations are from the Holy Bible, New International Version, 1973, 1978, 1984.

Quranic quotations are from The Meaning of the Holy Quran, New Edition with Revised Translation and Commentary, by Abdullah Yusuf Ali, 1989

First published in U.S.A. 1998 by Defenders Publications.
ISBN 0-910643-01-6

Contents

Introduction

ISLAM... perhaps one of the most familiar and important words in the vocabulary of the twentieth century, with continuing importance for the duration of the coming twenty-first century.

ISLAM... a word which conveys immediate meaning to nearly all the world population. To more than one billion, two hundred million people the word means hope, peace, justice, and compassion. To yet millions more, the word represents what they consider to be the greatest of threats to their peace, their freedom, and their modern way of life.

ISLAM... an Arabic word literally meaning "PEACE" and "SUBMISSION," representing the religious faith of nearly one fourth of the entire world population, and fast becoming the primary religion in Europe, Asia, the former Soviet Union, and the African continent.

COALITION OR COLLISION... Christianity and Islam continue to be the two fastest growing religions in the world. Men and women, both Christian and Muslim, are now asking the question, must these two religions collide? Is there no common ground between them? Many Muslims are taught that Christianity seeks to eliminate Islam; that Christians have no knowledge or understanding of their faith; that Christians condemn Islam, and hold the teachings of Islamic Fundamentalism responsible for many if not all the terrorist activities throughout the world.

Many Christians are taught that Islam teaches the worship of a false God; that Islam was and still is spread by force and terror; that all Muslims are Arabs, and that both oppose the policies of the United States and the essentials of democracy. Millions of Christians have been taught for decades that Islam is an intolerant religion, forbidding the free choice and practice of any other religion except Islam. By far the great majority of citizens of the West continue to teach, repeat and believe the distortions and prejudices created centuries ago by a European civilization which regarded Islam as the "traditional enemy."

False images of Islam were formed by literary accounts of Roland, El Cid, Don Juan at the Battle of Lepanto, and given exotically sinister coloring in lurid tales of harem intrigues, lascivious heavens, and dangerous casbahs. Textbooks on European civilization, then and now, presented Islam as the religion which put an end to the ancient centers of primitive Christianity in the Middle East and North Africa, replaced Christian Constantinople in the Eastern Mediterranean and the Balkans, and occupied Spain for almost 900 years.

Somehow omitted and forgotten are the fruitful scientific collaboration and theological discussions which occurred in Baghdad in the 9th and 10th centuries, where Christian and Muslim scholars worked together to translate and comment upon Greek philosophy and science. Omitted is the fact that under the Nordic rule in Sicily, the first translation of Arab philosophy was accomplished which would have profound effect and influence on the works of Albert the Great and the famous Christian scholar Thomas Aquinas.

Forgotten and omitted are the myriad of historical accounts of Christians and Muslims living and working together for the common good of their societies, as evidenced in the 9th century by the visit of Francis of Assisi to the Mamluk Sultan in Egypt at the height of the Crusades, and the 16th century dialogues between Christian and Muslim scholars organized at the initiative of the Mogul Emperor Akbar in modern India and Pakistan.

As a Christian who has lived, studied and interacted with Muslim believers for many years, it is both my pleasure and

serious responsibility to set forth the basic history and teachings of Islam, in an effort to educate the sincere individual
who truly wants to know what Muslims believe and practice,
and once learning these things, that individual may join with
other Christians in building bridges of peace, dialogue, and
understanding with the brothers and sisters of Islam.

I wish to express special thanks to Dr. Robert H. Schuller,
founder of the Crystal Cathedral in Garden Grove California
and the Hour of Power television program, for his personal
commitment and support for the establishment of CAMP,
Christians and Muslims for Peace. Dr. Schuller is a rare
example of a servant of God who lives and applies his faith
to the current needs and issues of the world. It was Dr.
Schuller who, understanding the realities and status of the
world today and in the coming twenty-first century, first
expressed the fear that we are, as Christians and Muslims,
headed towards either a collision or coalition. It is my prayer
that you, the reader, will join us in the pursuit of a coalition
whereby men and women who serve the living God of all
men and nations, might come together on common ground,
and in unity oppose the common evils of all mankind while
joining hands in the pursuit of peace, freedom, justice and
moral values.

Chapter One
Origins of Islam

In this chapter we will discover the origin and meaning of Islam, as well as a brief background of the life of Prophet Muhammed. Special focus will be upon the geographical and historical setting of the life and times of Muhammed which played a part In the beginning of Islam.

WHAT IS THE ORIGIN AND MEANING OF THE WORD "ISLAM"?

ISLAM literally means submission, obedience, or surrender, and is derived from the Arabic root "SLM" or in English Salam, which means peace. This same Arabic word can also mean purity and obedience, but its primary meaning is peace. Islam is pronounced with the accent on the second syllable: i-SLAM. A literal definition of Islam is "peace through submission to the will of Allah."

The Arabic word "Salam" is used in the world-wide greeting of every Muslim to another Muslim as well as true Christian believers: "Assalamu Alaykum," which means the peace of God be with or upon you. Thus we learn that the very meaning of the term "Islam" does not mean war, terror, aggression or intolerance, but PEACE! An acceptable understanding of peace in Islam is that one can achieve real peace of body and mind only through submission and obedience to God, and that such a life of obedience brings with it peace of the heart and establishes real peace in society at large. The concept of peace as taught in Islam is decidedly ignored or overlooked by contemporary media types and many Judaeo/Christian "scholars" who demonize Islam at every opportunity. Peace and Islam are derived from the same root and may be considered synonymous. The concluding of daily prayers of every Muslim are words of Peace. The greeting of Muslims and daily salutations are expressions of peace. Heaven in Islam is the "abode of peace." Islam teaches that the individual who approaches God as a Muslim cannot fail to be at peace with God, himself, and with his fellow man. Men of good faith and principles cannot fail to make the world a better world, to regain human dignity, to achieve equality, to enjoy universal brotherhood, and to build a lasting peace.

IS IT CORRECT TO CALL BELIEVERS IN ISLAM "MUHAMMADANS"?

Absolutely NOT! Islam is the name of the religion, and unlike Christianity, Buddhism, and other religions of the world, is not named after its founder. To call Islam "Muhammadanism" would be like calling Christianity "St. Paulism." Believers of Islam believe God, not Muhammad founded their religion. Muhammad played a crucial role in the formulation of Islam, but he is secondary to God and the Quran in terms of importance and status. Muhammad is not divine nor an incarnation of God, and is not worshiped in any manner whatsoever.

WHAT DOES "MUSLIM" MEAN?

Muslim means "one surrendered or submitted to God." The person who practices Islam is a Muslim (male) or Muslima (female). By definition, any individual who is totally submitted and obedient to the will of God, is considered a Muslim. Thus the religion of Islam considers Abraham and all the Prophets of the Bible as Muslims. This author has presented lectures in numerous Islamic Centers and Mosques, and has many times been called a Muslim. Thus true Christians seeking to obey the laws and commandments of God are, in one sense, Muslims.

> *"Say, we believe in Allah and in what has been revealed to Abraham, Ishmael, Isaac, Jacob, and the tribes, in what was given to Moses and Jesus, and in what the prophets received from their Lord; we make no distinction between any of them."* (Holy Quran 2:136)

However, the term Muslim as used and understood in its most restrictive sense today refers to one who has made a two-pronged confession or declaration called "Shahadah," an Arabic word meaning "witnessing."

> *"There is no God but God, and Muhammad is the Prophet of God."*

This statement or affirmation, in its entirety, along with an attempt to truly live a righteous life, distinguishes the Muslim who submits to God, and a Muslim who follows the tenets and teachings of Islam.

WHO WAS MUHAMMAD?
WHERE AND WHEN DID HE LIVE?

Muhammad, whose name in Arabic means "the highly praised one," was born in the Arabian town and commercial center named Mecca (Makka in Arabic). The exact date of his birth is disputed, but most generally agreed to be around the year A.D. 570. Such uncertainty is not unusual in the Middle East; for instance, it is hard to date the birth of the famous Abdal Aziz ibn-Saud (known as ibn-Saud) the conqueror and unifier of Arabia, a man who ruled for more than fifty years, died in 1953, and whose personality, conduct, and biography are known in great detail.

Muhammad was the son of a young couple of the Quraysh tribe and the Banu Hashim clan, born on the twelfth day of the third lunar month of Islam's calendar (see Glossary for information on meaning of lunar calendar). His father, Abdullah, died two months before his birth, and his mother, Aminah, died when he was six years of age. Both his parents came from a background of nobility and community leadership. His grandfather, Abdal Muttalib, was a "hakam" or arbiter, a custodian of the Kabah, a cube-shaped building in Mecca built by Abraham as the first house of worship, the "Holy of Holies" for Muslim pilgrims and the place toward which all Muslim prayers are directed. He was also the virtual head of the Meccan commonwealth. Upon his grandfathers death he was adopted by his uncle, Abu-Talib.

Little is recorded or known of his youth, but as an orphan raised in Mecca which was located in the middle of the trade artery between Jordan, Syria, and Lebanon, his was a world of color and excitement, of camel caravans, foreign languages, constant scenes of barter, visits to the shrine of the Black Stone in the Kabah, and the din of soothsayers and poets. A young Muhammad traveled with his uncle's caravans to northern Arabia and Syria, and it was on these same "business trips" that he learned and enhanced his business acumen and diplomatic skills. These skills came to the attention of a woman named Khadijah, a wealthy widow who was quite successful in a variety of business ventures including a trading company and caravans. Khadijah hired Muhammad and he eventually became the supervisor of her commercial enterprises. Although she was at the age of forty, and Muhammad fifteen years her junior at twenty-five, they were married.

Their marriage produced six children, two boys who died in infancy, and four girls. Only the youngest daughter

Fatima outlived her father. It is noteworthy to point out to the critics of Islam, that Muhammad remained married to this one individual wife for a period of twenty-five years until her death, despite the fact that polygamy was an acceptable cultural practice of the entire region. In the year 620 and at the age of fifty, severe sadness and sorrow swept into Muhammad's life with the death of both his uncle Talib and his beloved wife Khadijah.

RECITE! THE NIGHT OF POWER!

Muhammad had for several years made a practice of seeking a quiet place for solitude, contemplation and reflection. He found such a location in a cave on Mt. Hira, on the outskirts of Mecca. It was here, at the age of forty that a voice pierced the coolness of the evening saying:

"Proclaim (or Read) in the name of your Lord and Cherisher who created man out of a (mere) clot of Clay. Proclaim!" (Surah 15:28)

So began the revelation of the angel Gabriel to Muhammad. Over a period of the next twenty-three years, until his death in the year A.D. 632, Islam teaches that God, through the angel Gabriel, communicated the words of the Quran to Muhammad. Muhammad died of fever June 8, 632 in the arms of his wife Aisha and was buried in their home in the city of Yathrib which was thereafter called al Madinah. (Medina)

The life and times of Muhammad are extremely important, thus I have included in the Suggested Reading section some of the very best resources on the life of Prophet Muhammad. He was of a certainty a most unique and special man who demonstrated within his own life the virtues of humility, compassion, obedience, and a thirst for justice, and a call for all men to worship the one and only God of all creation.

Never did Muhammad claim any form of deity, nor did he ask for or command reverence or special recognition for himself. The Message of Muhammad was, and remains to this day, a message of Peace, Mercy, and Compassion. His was a message of tolerance and peaceful coexistence, as we shall discover in Chapter 3. We will close this brief study of his life and death with the words of Abu-Bakr, who became one of the earliest believers in the message of Muhammad and who was a popular and respected merchant of Mecca, and who later became the very first Caliph (successor). The task of announcing the death of Muhammad to a massive throng which had gathered outside the Prophet's home was left to Abu-Bakr. From his words to that gathering, it is clear that from the very beginning, Muslim believers understood that Muhammad was, like all Prophets before him, mortal flesh.

"O Muslims! If any of you has been worshipping Muhammad, then let me tell you Muhammad is dead. But if you really do worship God, then know that God is living and will never die."

Chapter Two
History of Islam

HOW AND WHY DID ISLAM BEGIN
TO TAKE ROOT AND SPREAD?

ISLAM BEGAN IN ARABIA as Muhammad was an Arab living in the city of Mecca. The word "Arab" is derived from the Semitic word "arav" meaning nomad. Traditionally, Arab is said to derive from the little town of Araba in the southeast district of the Tihamah, where, according to legend, settled Ya'rab, son of the Biblical Joktan. It was Ya'rab who imparted his name to the peninsula and its inhabitants. (see Genesis 10:25, 26, 29)

The earliest civilizations of Arabia included the Minaean, Sabaean, and the Himyarite. From the second millennium B.C. until the arrival of Islam in the seventh century A.D. these civilizations thrived mainly on agriculture and trade. Politically, the Arabians had established a theocratic-aristo-cratic form of government which Islam did not alter.

Mass emigrations from Arabia occurred, such as one recorded in 535 B.C. following the breach of the great dam at Ma'rib. From the third millennium B.C. onward, at intervals of every five-hundred years, mass migrations from Arabia northward accounted for the earliest civilizations in Syria and Mesopotamia: Amorite, Akkadian, Canaanite, Phoenician, Aramaean, Hebrew, Nabataean, Ghassanid, and lastly, the Muslim Arab. These civilizations form the basis of the nine Semitic Tribes from which descended various semit-ical nations including the Caananites, Amorites, and Hebrews whose struggles are portrayed in the biblical text.

Earliest history confirms that Arabia occupied a medieval position geographically between the ancient centers of astonishing civilization in the Mesopatamian, Nile, and Indus valleys, the western Indian littoral, and the Ethiopian highlands. The Arabians became "middle-men" for trade since some of the best trade routes traversed the Arabian peninsula. I suggest the interested reader pursue further reading on the cultural and tribal background of the Arabic people, since some of the customs and practices were, quite naturally, a part of early Islam.

WHAT WAS THE EARLY RELIGIOUS BACKGROUND OF ARABIA?

Pre-Islamic religion in Arabia was a mixture of certain deities and cultic rituals associated with animism and daeimonism. However, there is some anthropological evidence that monotheism, sanctified stones and springs such as the Black Stone of the Kabah in Islam, and the well of Zamzam, offering of blood sacrifices, and numerous religious rites later adopted and practiced in Judaism, Christianity, and Islam, were present in pre-Islamic Arabia.

The tribes of Arabia selected those deities which reflected their distinguishing characteristics and aspirations. These Semites created their gods in their own images, and the mood and temperament of the god was a direct reflection of its maker and worshipper. Pagan Arabia contained hundreds of gods, and even the Kabah at one time housed three hundred and sixty-seven of them. Although the time of the Old Testament Prophets and New Testament Apostles had long since passed, both Christianity and Judaism had influenced the region, but by the sixth century A.D. false and pagan worship had set in to such an extent that even the God of the Bible had been reduced to the 'god of gods" in the pantheon of Arabic gods. Thus Allah, which to the Arabians means "the god", also called Il (god) by the Babylonians, "El" (god) by the Canaanites and later the Israelites, was considered the "father" of three of the more popular gods mentioned in the Quran, including al-Uzza (power), Lat (the goddess), and Manah (fate).

Much of the information concerning the myths, symbols, and rituals of the time is found in the condemnation of them by the Quran. The Quran refers to pre-Islamic Arabia as a "time of ignorance" (Jahiliyyah). Particularly prevalent was the practice of animism, which basically advocates that all aspects of nature possess sacred powers; everything is animated, full of life, or inhabited with spiritual forces. A perfect example was the veneration of stones, viewed by animists as providing protection from animals, shade from the desert sun, and building stones for shelters and homes. This may account for the Black Stone kept in the Kabah which was believed to be a meteorite which fell to earth centuries before and placed in the corner of the Kabah as a foundation stone by Abraham himself. One can understand how such a climate of paganism could prove fertile ground for the birth of such legends. The Black Stone legend was of such concern to Omar the second Caliph of Islam that he wanted to remove it from the wall of the Kabah completely. Legends die hard, and even today Muslims retain the old practice of touching and kissing the Black Stone as a part of the pilgrimage to Mecca, though there is no sacredness or divinity associated with the stone whatsoever.

WHAT IS THE HISTORICAL LINK BETWEEN ISLAM, JUDAISM, AND CHRISTIANITY?

Judaism and Christianity existed in Arabia many centuries prior to the birth of Muhammad. Separate communities of Jews and Christians settled primarily in western and southern Arabia. Jews and Christians were the predominant businessmen in Medina. By the time of Muhammad's birth, one-half of Medina's population was comprised of Jews. The presence of Jewish tribes dates back to 1200 B.C. when those tribes descended from Rachel wandered in the Sinai. Between the years 132-135 A.D, after a second disastrous failed uprising against Rome, much of the Jewish population fled to the Medina/Mecca area of Arabia. Bringing with them a superior knowledge of agriculture coupled with business skills, they quickly became the most prosperous and powerful of the resident population. Muhammad interacted with the Jewish citizens often and early in his proclamation of the message received from Gabriel, calling the Jews the "People of the Book" (Ahl al-Kitab), meaning the Bible.

CHRISTIANITY WAS ALSO PRESENT in the area but had less impact on Islam due to the fact that the primary Christian centers were located on the periphery of the peninsula north of Yemen, in Syria and lower Iraq. We do have an archaeological/historical record of a small Christian community thriving in Mecca prior to the birth of Islam as well as during the lifetime of Prophet Muhammad. This community consisted of caravan leaders, monks, merchants, doctors and dentists, blacksmiths, carpenters, and intellectuals such as teachers, orators, and scribes.

The Apostle Paul's mission to Damascus firmly established Christianity in Syria, the land area directly to the north of Arabia. Historical evidence reveals that the outreach of the early Christian community in Syria was successful and extended to the area of Mecca. Archaeological evidence for a relatively small but important Christian community is affirmed by ancient artist's drawings of Jesus and his mother Mary on the inner walls of the Kabah.

A variety of dissident Christian monks, primarily of the Monophysite confession along with other acetic monks located their retreats in the steppes of north Arabia in the midst of the popular caravan routes. Persistent oral tradition asserts that Muhammad, as a caravan leader, became friends with one of these monks named Bahira, and that he even wore tunics that were gifts from other Christian monks. Two Arab tribes of Christians, the Judham and the Udhra roamed the region. Monasteries lining the caravan routes were open and available to the roaming Bedouins as well as the numerous travelling caravans. It is noteworthy that ancient monastery records reveal that the frequent visitors not only received food and shelter, but were directly exposed to the daily practice of prayer, fasting, and the giving of alms, three of the five basic tenets of Islam. Thus Judaism and Christianity prepared the way for the Quran's message of monotheism. Those listening to Muhammad would be familiar with his call to recognize and worship the One True God of all mankind!

DID ISLAM SPREAD THROUGH FEAR, FORCE, AND WARFARE?

This question is worthy of a separate volume alone since nearly every university class on comparative religion has consistently stressed the concept of Islamic "Jihad" or Holy War, advocating that Islam was spread by threat of death. This author recalls his own college professor becoming flushed with rage and indignity, with elevated voice and a clenched fist, stressing over and over again to the class that conversion to Islam was never of free will or volition, but one and all were held by the hair and with a sword to their throat, were given the choice: "Islam or the sword?" Every student left that class and later, that university, prejudiced and hostile to the religion of Islam without even knowing the tenets and teachings of Islam, and most assuredly the historical facts. Not once during the entire semester were we referred or encouraged to read the

Quran or any of the massive historical documents and records of the past centuries detailing the spread of Islam. Sadly, not much has changed in the Western educational systems, and bias and prejudice continue to abound, distortions and exaggerations reign supreme, especially in light of the developments of the twentieth century which has witnessed the rediscovery and revitalization of a living, dynamic Islam. This contemporary Islam is challenging the economic and political status quo of the past one hundred years, and is viewed by the western nations and population as a serious threat to their own continued global domination.

Through his own words, we find that Muhammad had no intention of founding a new religion. His entire goal was to enlist his fellow Arabs to recognize and worship one God, the only God, as worshipped by their neighbors, the Christians and Jews. Muhammad did not view his mission and message as superseding those of his predecessors, from Abraham to Jesus, but rather as serving to complete and revitalize these two great religions.

The Jews in Medina warmly received Muhammad at first, for as we shall see in the next chapter, he had included Abraham, Moses, and the Torah in his vision. The Jews were his brothers and sisters, and to show his solidarity, the early Muslims were asked to face Jerusalem when they prayed. Later, when the Jews did not accept Islam or convert to the new religion, mistrust and suspicion became the norm, and when the Jews formed military alliances with enemies of Muhammad, he expelled them from Medina and asked his followers to stop praying toward Jerusalem and turn instead to Mecca. Muhammad saw himself as the liberator and protector of Judaism and Christianity, and he believed that his message would help resolve the disputes between the Jews and Christians of Arabia.

"The Jews say the Christians follow nothing (true), and the Christians say the Jews follow nothing (true); yet both are readers of the Scripture. Even thus speak those who know not. Allah will judge between them on the Day of Resurrection concerning that wherein they differ." (Surah 2:113.)

The early years of Islam during the lifetime of the Prophet were full of rejection, unbelief, false accusations, and eventually, tribal conflicts with those who wanted to retain the old pagan gods and forms of worship. Remember, even the Kabah was filled with some 360 idols. Following the death of Muhammad, the expansion of Islam is without parallel in religious history. Having been successful in making his native land an Islamic country in his lifetime, Islam quickly spread from Arabia north to Damascus, and within the next twenty years, to Jerusalem, east to Persia, west to Egypt, and eventually the African continent. By the year 715 A.D., a mere one hundred years into the new Islamic era, Islam was predominant and in control of the Mediterranean Sea and the European country of Spain. By 800, Muslims controlled land from Switzerland to the eastern regions of India, a land area larger than the great Roman Empire at its zenith. The spread of Islam continued into the twelfth century, and once again emerged with renewed vigor in the sixteenth-century thanks in part to the great Ottoman empire. It is true that many battles were fought down through the centuries between Muslims and Christians, but I suggest the reader pursue the study of those wars and conflicts by a careful reading of history, and some of the books and resources listed under the Suggested Reading List section of this book. Suffice it to say that numerous wrongs and acts of barbarity were committed in the name of God and Church as men, both Muslim and Christian, often failed to practice the very heart and soul of their own religions.

It is a matter of historical record that many of the people "conquered" by Islam practically welcomed the change, after centuries of tyrannical rule by Byzantine Emperors and Persian Kings. Conquered people were called Dhimmis, non-Muslims who were guaranteed tolerance by Islamic law. Jews and Christians, both called "People of the Book" in the Quran, were given special treatment. All Dhimmis were permitted to retain their own religious and civil rights, and for this privilege, a tax, similar to a state tax of today, was levied against them.

Perhaps the best illustration of tolerance and peaceful co-existence envisaged by Muhammad is the Charter of Medina, which, under the guidance and inspiration of Muhammad, was a covenant between the Jews, Muslims, and other inhabitants of the city which guaranteed religious liberty and determined the rights and duties of members of all religions. True Islam, like true Christianity and Judaism, places a premium on Peace, Justice, and Compassion.

"Let there be no compulsion in religion: Truth stands out from Error; Whoever rejects Evil and believes in God has grasped the most trustworthy handhold, that never breaks. And God hears and knows all things." (Surah 2:256)

Chapter Three
The Quran and Pillars of Islamic Faith

In this chapter we will discover the background of the Quran, including its origin, composition, and authorship. We will then examine the five primary tenets or "pillars" of Islam practiced by more than one billion, two hundred million Muslim believers around the world.

WHAT IS THE QURAN, AND HOW AND WHEN DID IT APPEAR?

The word Quran is Arabic meaning "recitation." It is known as the "al-Kitab" (the book) of Allah. The Quran is the written revelations of the angel Gabriel delivered to Muhammad while in Medina and Mecca spanning a twenty-three year period between the years 610 and 632 A.D. The process of delivery between Gabriel and Muhammad is called "tanzil" in Arabic, which literally means "causing to descend." The Quran was given in the Arabic language since it was intended for the people of Arabia, and Muhammad himself was an Arab. Although the Quran has been translated into other languages, all Muslim believers must learn to read and understand Arabic in order to gain a full understanding of the Quran.

DIDN'T MUHAMMAD WRITE THE QURAN?

Muhammad was illiterate and therefore, DID NOT WRITE THE QURAN! He recited the teachings he received from Gabriel to those who would listen, and eventually over the period of his lifetime, some thirty thousand adherents had memorized the complete set of revelations. Those who memorize the Quran are called the "Huffaz." Soon after his death, his successor Abu Bakr, the first Caliph, (which means successor) collected all the revelations which many followers had written down to preserve the purity of the text and to enable them to share the message with others. Abu Bakr bound all of these together forming one document. Versions of this first edition occurred when the message of Islam was proclaimed to other regions, including Syria, Iraq, and Persia.

The fact that Arabic was the original language of the Quran has served to protect it from suffering the fate of many other books, including the changing of word meanings, the addition of scribal comments into the text, etc. Because of the organic affinity of Arabic with the divine revelation to Muhammad, Arabic has not changed since the Quranic text was completed. Quranic Arabic remains today, some fourteen centuries later, standard Arabic containing the norms of grammar and syntactical usage among all contemporary Arabs. Within twenty years following the death of Muhammad, under the guidance of the third Caliph named Uthman whose Caliphate lasted from 644 until 656, the Quran was canonized into its present form. This became the "authorized version" and has remained the same to this day. During the same period, the numbering, titling, and ordering of chapters were added to the Quran for the very first time.

THE QURAN IS COMPRISED of chapters and verses, and is nearly the same size as the New Testament. Each chapter is called a "surah" which means step or gradation. The reader symbolically ascends closer to Allah as he continues to study and read the Quran. The Quran contains 114 surahs, 6,616 verses, 77,934 words, and 323,671 letters. Every chapter of the Quran with the exception of Surah 9 begins with the "Bismillah," the core of Islamic faith:

> *"Bismillah-ir-Raham-ir-Rahim"... In the Name of God, the Most Compassionate, the Most Merciful."*

Surahs vary in length from 287 verses to only 3 verses. The verses themselves are of unequal length; some consist of only two words, while others run for nearly half a page. Each surah received a title generally dealing with a particular subject. The act of titling dates back to the second Muslim century. Dividing the Quranic text into four, eight, or thirty parts for a total of sixty sections was done for the practical purpose of committing the Quran to memory. The longest surahs appear first and relate to the period of Muhammad's role as head of the community in Medina, while the shorter ones pay specific attention to ethical teachings during his stay in Mecca. Each surah usually ends with the epitaph "Meccan" or "Medinan" to indicate the location of revelation.

The Quran is the infallible Word of God to Muslim believers. Muslims believe it is an exact replication of the "Book of Books" which forever rests by the side of God. The Quran holds the same place in Islam that Jesus holds for Christianity. Therefore, when you read the Quran it is as if God is reading to you. To insult, defame, or trivialize the Quran is to do the same to God himself. That is why the perverted ramblings of Salman Rushdie's "Satanic Verses" were so offensive to the entire world of Islam.

DO MUSLIMS HAVE OTHER BOOKS BESIDES THE QURAN?

MUHAMMAD WAS A MORTAL like the rest of humanity as we have already discovered in the first chapter. But since he lived a life pleasing to God and served his fellow Muslims well, his sayings and doings, manners and customs, his answers to questions on religious life and faith, and, above all his decisions in legal disputes became a source of important reference for both layman and jurist, rebel and law keeper, philosopher and theologian. As a result, two separate books were written which, although non-canonical, are second only to the Quran in the Islamic hierarchy of authority. They are not considered part of the revelation of God, nor to be included in or on a par with, the Quran. THE HADITH... which means speech or utterances, and the SUNNAH which means conduct or acts, were the written observations of eye-witnesses who accompanied Muhammad during the twenty-three years he received the Quran. Often Hadith and Sunna are used interchangeably when referring to an act or word of the Prophet. This is especially true today in any discussion of the Shariah, the fundamental law or constitution of Islam. Hundreds of thousands of hadiths were attributed to Muhammad after his death, and it was not until nearly two centuries after his death that a serious attempt was made to determine their validity. Among the many who attempted this feat was a Muslim named al-Bukhari who spent sixteen years journeying through Muslim lands to collect more than 600,000 hadiths. His work is considered the most important to Muslims today, and contains some 4,000 hadiths. An example of how the Hadith is viewed and utilized by Muslims today might be illustrated by saying the Quran tells the Muslim he should pray, while the Hadith shows him how; the Quran tells him to fast, the Hadith gives him the details of Ramadan, a sacred month requiring every Muslim to fast from dawn to sunset daily. The Quran is the Truth and Word of God, the Hadith is the wisdom and example of the Prophet Muhammad.

WHAT DOES ISLAM TEACH ABOUT GOD, AND IS ALLAH THE SAME AS THE GOD IN THE BIBLE?

ALLAH is the Syriac and Arabic name for God. In ancient Babylon the name was il, and then with the Hebrews became "El" (Elohim). El came into the Arabic with the definite article IL-ah and then into the English as Allah with a literal

meaning of "THE GOD, one to be worshipped." The some-
times intentional distortions and accusations implying that
Allah is only the God of Muslims, or a false god of the old
Babylonian era is totally without historical merit. Even primary reference works of today tend to repeat the anti-Islamic
propaganda as evidenced by the following quote taken from
Webster's New Collegiate Dictionary, 1973:

"ALLAH: the Supreme Being of the Muslims."
I refer the reader to the previous chapter where we clearly
understood that the call of Islam to a pagan and multi-god
Arabia and surrounding region was for all men to forgo their
numerous gods, and come to a position of worship of the
One God of All Men and Nations, not the god of all other
gods. Allah, the God of Islam, is the same Jehovah, Elohim, of
Judaism and Christianity. The God of Islam and the Quran is
the same omniscient, omnipresent, creator God of the Bible.

*La ilaha illa Allah, wa Muhammad rasul Allah "There is no
god but Allah and Muhammad is the prophet of Allah."*

TAWHID:…. unity with God. The foundation of Islam is the
uncompromising unity and oneness of God, called Tawhid in
the Arabic language. Allah is beyond distinction and divi-
sion, and has no equal or associate. Although God is One,
there are many names for God. In fact, the Quran lists ninety-
nine "most beautiful names of God." (Surah 7:180)
Among these names we find: Creator, All-Merciful,
Guardian of Faith, All-Holy, All-Wise, Just, Beautiful, Loving,
Compassionate, and Glorious. The remaining names can be
found by reading Surah 59:224 and 2:255 along with the
names contained in the Hadith. Another misnomer among
the uninformed concerning Islam is the constantly repeated

statement that Muslims carry "worry beads" in their hands which they rub their fingers over in "nervous" situations. Many have likened the beads to the prayer beads of Roman Catholicism. All are wrong. The Subha is a prayer thread consisting of thirty-three beads and a tassel. As the Muslim believer runs each bead through his or her fingers, they repeat one of the names for God. Repeating this process three times enables the person to recite all ninety-nine names of God. I have seen Muslims all over the world at work and at play, day and night, forever caressing their Subha, earnestly desiring to have the presence of God within their heart, soul, and consciousness.

The Unity or Tawhid of Allah is reflected in the unity of the creation and order of the world. This includes the unity of the human family. Islam teaches that all people are members of one single family of God, hence all are related, since all men are created by God, and He alone is the Provider for all men, the Judge of all men, and the Lord of all men. We are all of one family with regard to our creation, our original parentage, and our final destiny. The call of Islam is a call of inclusiveness on the basis of universal appeal. Understanding the unity of God helps us understand how Islam transcends all diversity, including racial, ethnic, and nationality. Islam holds there are no distinctions or separations between church and state, economics and religion, or religion and politics. Being a true practicing Muslim means that life in totality is lived with the absolute Lordship of God. The revealed and expressed will and attitude of God is to be recognized and applied in all the venues of life, and in no way restricted or limited to "religious" activities only. There is no facet of life, no hidden or private corner within ones being that is free from the admonitions and constraints of God.

WHAT ARE THE FIVE TENETS OR "PILLARS" OF ISLAM?

Islam is like a house built on the rock of submission and supported by five pillars: Witnessing, Prayer, Fasting, Almsgiving or Tithing, and Pilgrimage. These five pillars are the distinguishing marks of Islam from all other religions. Every Muslim everywhere in the world must practice and observe these five pillars. There is no such thing as a "nominal" or "non-practicing" or "non-religious" Muslim as is also true of Judaism and Christianity.

I. SHAHADAH... An Arabic word meaning "witnessing." All five pillars appear as a unit but the one pillar which stands in the middle and around which all the rest revolve is Shahadah.

> "There is no God but God, and Muhammad is the Prophet of God."

This testimony is considered the most important declaration a Muslim can make; it is accepted as evidence of one converted to Islam, as well as what helps make one a Muslim. This phrase is the first few words whispered into the ear of a newborn baby, and the last words from the lips of the dying. No other phrase or words are repeated more frequently then these. They are repeated by believers on the average of twenty times each day. There are five main elements in Islamic faith which are subsumed under Shahadah:

(1) Belief in one God who alone is worthy of worship.
(2) Belief in angels which do the will of God.
(3) Belief in sacred books including the Torah (Taurah) and the Gospel (Injil), all inspired by God.

(4) Belief in the Prophets as examples to follow and as spokesmen of God.

(5) Belief in the Day of Judgment and the Resurrection.

II. SALAH... An Arabic word for prayer. One of the most familiar images of Islam in the Western world is that of men in a mosque bowing and prostrating in union. This is Salat or worship, of which Salah or prayer is at the very center. Muslims are required to pray five times daily which may be offered from any location. This author has observed Muslims praying on buses, barren hills and wilderness, in automobiles, the floors of airplanes in route, in the midst of exploding bombs, and in prisons. The prayers are to be made at specific times of each day, and are preceded by the call to prayer by the "muezzin" or one who calls to remind the faithful that the moment for prayer is at hand. I have heard the call to prayer around the world, and the form of the call is universal:

> *"God is great (four times). I bear witness that there is no God but God (twice). I bear witness that Muhammad is the messenger of God (twice). Come to prayer (twice). Come to contentment (twice). There is no God but God."*

The only time a Muslim is obligated to pray with fellow Muslims is at the noon service on Friday, which is indeed the recognized day of worship in Islam. This day is not, as in Judaism and some Christian denominations, considered a "Sabbath" or day of rest as stated in Surah 62:9,10:

> *"O You who believe! When the call is heard for the prayer of the day of congregation, haste unto remembrance of Allah and leave your trading...and when the prayer is ended, then disperse in the land and seek of Allah's bounty."*

The purpose of prayer in Islam is to increase one's consciousness of God, to purify the heart, to control temptation,
and to inspire one another to a higher morality. If a mosque is
unavailable, a prayer rug can serve as a replacement. Each
rug will have a point in its design to orient the prayer to
Mecca. If a Muslim is without a prayer rug, he can pray any
place that is clean. As the Prophet said:

"The entire earth has been made a mosque for me."

Before Salah (prayer) and Salat (worship) begin, ceremo-
nial bathing or cleansing is required. Mosques around the
world maintain circular fountains in the forecourt for this
purpose. Since most mosques in the western world do not
have such fountains, adequately equipped rest rooms provide the same services. The purpose of the outward cleansing
is to remind one of the serious nature of prayer before God. A
Muslim must enter prayer as purified from the defilement of
daily life and living as possible. The bathing of the body
implies the purity of the soul. The symbolic washing of the
ears demonstrates the desire to put away the words and
thoughts which surrounds the petitioner in daily living.

The five daily prayers are observed as follows:

(1) FAJR... Early morning prayer, before the sunrise.
(2) ZUHR... Noon prayer, between mid-day and sunset.
(3) ASR... Between three and five in the afternoon.
(4) MAGHRIB... After sunset, before darkness.
(5) ISHA... Evening prayer, any hour of darkness.

III. SAWM... An Arabic word for fasting, the third of the
five pillars of Islam. Prayer and fasting, the second and third
pillars are practiced in nearly every religion of the world. In
Islam, unlike the teaching in Christianity, fasting is primarily
reserved for the month of Ramadan. This is the ninth month

of the Islamic lunar calendar, and it is the month that Muslims believe Muhammad received the first revelations from God. Since Ramadan arrives at different times during the year, the length of the fast will vary, with shorter days in winter and longer hot days of the summer.

FASTING DURING RAMADAN requires the daily abstinence from all food, drink (including water), sexual activity, and all manner of pleasures to the senses such as music, etc. The fast begins before the break of dawn and ends immediately after sunset. The purpose of fasting is to practice self-denial, while at the same time to learn anew an appreciation for the simple gifts of God, food and drink. It also causes one to focus upon the plight of the many in the world who live daily lives without even these most basic necessities. It is intended as a time when the spiritual values of love, honesty, devotion, generosity, and concern for the poorest of society are heightened.

The daily fast is broken at sunset when the family shares a light meal known as Iftar meaning break-fast. Some two hours before sunrise the meal for the day is taken. At the end of Ramadan there is a festive celebration known as Eid Al-Fitr meaning Feast of the Breaking of the Fast. This celebration often includes family reunions and exchanging gifts.

IV. ZAKAT, an Arabic word meaning purity, but the intent and application of the term in Islam is to purify one's material possessions through regular proportional giving or sharing with the poor. Zakat is required of every Muslim and is the fourth pillar of Islamic faith. As one gives of his possessions to others, his heart is purified from selfishness and greed for wealth. Likewise, the one who receives assistance is freed from a heart of envy or jealousy. Like true Christianity, Islam teaches that believers own nothing in life, but everything they possess has been given to them by God in trust; they are trustees.

Zakat requires a minimum of two-and-one half percent of the total wealth of an individual. This is beyond any donations to charity or contributions for other needs during the year. The primary purpose of Zakat is to help the poor, other needy Muslims, and new converts to Islam.

Zakat could be considered a type of social security and welfare program combined for the needs of the poor. The author has often felt that the churches of Christianity could and should have enacted such a program long ago instead of the responsibility falling upon the government. An early Muslim leader once said of Zakat:

"Prayer carries us halfway to God; fasting brings us to the door of His praises; almsgiving procures for us admission."

V. HAJJ... Arabic for "pilgrimage," which is the fifth and final pillar of Islam. Every Muslim is required to make a pilgrimage to the sacred mountains of Mecca at least once in a lifetime, if they are physically and financially able to do so. The first two pillars dealt with daily duties, the second two annual obligations; the fifth pillar is considered the most noble act of worship and the crowning event in life. The Hajj is observed the twelfth month of the year, about sixty days following the conclusion of Ramadan. The rites during Hajj are performed from the eighth to the thirteenth of "Dhu'l Hajja" the last month of the Islamic calendar.

WHY DO THE MUSLIMS MAKE THE HAJJ OR PILGRIMAGE?

The purpose of the Hajj is to visit Mecca and the very first house of worship built by Abraham, the Kabah. Also, Islam teaches that Abraham's wife Hagar and her son Ishmael were abandoned in the wild, remote, mountainous region of Mecca. The angel Gabriel, hearing their cry for water, caused a spring to burst forth from a well that exists to this day called Zamzam. The city of Mecca was built adjacent to this rare source of water. Muslim pilgrims visit the well and recall the plight of Hagar and Ishmael, and drink from its refreshing depths.

Another act by the pilgrim involves the circling of the Kabah seven times, praying to God and reciting the Quran. The number seven is used since seven is considered a holy number in the Bible. It represents perfection, wholeness, and completeness. The Kabah is 40 feet long, 33 feet wide, and 50 feet high. It is covered with a black cloth with verses from the Quran embroidered in gold thread. The four corners of the Kabah align with the four points of the compass. Other ritual acts accompany the pilgrimage, including the visiting of Mina, where the sacrifice of Ishmael was to occur, and to the Mount of Mercy, where Prophet Muhammad delivered his last sermon.

Many pilgrims go to Medina to visit Muhammad's Tomb and the Prophet's Mosque. A complete Hajj has the pilgrim going to Jerusalem to visit the "Farthest Mosque" which is called the Al-Aqsa on the temple mount to observe what is termed Muhammad's "Night Journey."

The Hajj serves as a symbol of the unity of Islam, and perhaps best explains the attraction of so many diverse nationalities, races, and cultures to the call of Islam. At Hajj every Muslim is equal and none are elevated above another. As millions upon millions gather as one massive congregation, old prejudices and racial barriers vanish; men or women, rich or poor, literate or illiterate, powerful or weak, ruler or ruled, Arab or non-Arab, they stand as one, each in the identical simple unsewn robe of white cloth, each standing and bowing and in one voice declaring:

"Labbaik, Allahumma Labbaik, Doubly at Your service, O God, Doubly at Your service."

Chapter Four
Islam and Christianity: Common Ground Between Us

WHAT DOES ISLAM TEACH ABOUT THE BIBLE?

The reader will recall in Chapter three that of the five main elements falling under the cover of Shahadah, number three was belief in the sacred books including the Torah and the Gospel. Few Christians are aware that Prophet Muhammad, the messenger of Islam, believed Jesus and Moses were the most important bearers of God's revelation to mankind, and that message is enshrined in the Torah and New Testament. Islam embraces both books and includes portions of both in the text of the Quran. As Christians believe the New Testament was the completion of the Old Testament of Judaism, so Muslims believe Islam and the Quran serve as the final completion of both books, and Muhammad as the last Prophet or Messenger of God.

Both the Torah and the New Testament are viewed by Islam as inspired revelation of God to mankind. Both Jews and Christians are referred to in the Quran as "People of the Book" meaning the Bible.

> *"And dispute not with the people of the Book except with means better than mere disputation, unless it be with those of them who inflict wrong and injury: But say, 'We believe in the Revelation which has come down to us and in that which came down to you; Our God and your God is One; and it is to Him we bow in Islam." (Surah 29:46)*

The Quran calls upon Muslims to attempt to sit down peacefully with People of the Book in an effort to find the common ground between them.

"Say: 'O People of the Book! Come to common terms as between us and you; that we worship none but Allah; that we associate no partners with Him; that we erect not from among ourselves lords and patrons other than Allah.'" (Surah 3:64)

Clearly, Islam teaches that no Prophet, Apostle, Saint or other human being is to be venerated or worshipped in any form or manner. Islam views the placing of any human being between God and mankind as wrong and misguided, including the intercessory positions of some saints as practiced by a variety of churches and denominations. Again, the Quran repeatedly states the clear acceptance of the Bible, with special emphasis upon the Old Testament Prophets, the Torah, first five lawbooks, and portions of the New Testament or gospel.

"Say: 'We believe in Allah, and in what has been revealed to us and what was revealed to Abraham,Ishmael, Isaac, Jacob, and the Tribes, and in the books given to Moses, Jesus, and the Prophets from their Lord. We make no distinction between one and another."(Sur3:84)

Muslims are asked to follow the good examples of the earlier Prophets of the Bible.

"The same religion has He established for you as that which He enjoined on Noah. That which we have sent by inspiration to you and that which we enjoined on Abraham, Moses and Jesus; namely, that you should remain steadfast in religion, and make no divisions. To those who worship other things than Allah hard is the way to which you call them. Allah chooses to Himself those whom He pleases, and guides to Himself those who turn to Him." (Surah 42:13)

The Quran clearly states that a Muslim may even marry pure women of the Book, as well as partake of their food as recorded in Surah 5:5:

> *"This day all things good and pure are made lawful for you. The food of the People of the Book is lawful for you, and yours is lawful for them. Also lawful for you to marry are not only pure women who are believers, but pure women from among the People of the Book."*

ALTHOUGH THE JEWS joined with the enemies of early Islam, neither they nor Judaism were targeted by Muhammad or Islam. It is a fact of history that when the Jews were being persecuted in Europe during the middle ages they found peace, harmony, and acceptance among the Muslim people of Spain. In fact, this was the era of Jewish history that they themselves refer to as "the golden age." In the famous treatise by Rabbi Minken he says of this era:

> *"It was Muslim Spain, the only land the Jew knew in nearly a thousand years of their dispersion, which made the genius of physician Moses Maimonides possible."*

After the fall of Spain, the Jews followed the Muslims to Morocco and to Egypt, where Maimonides became the personal physician to the great Muslim leader Saladin, who sent him to King Richard in order to treat the king. During the Ottoman period and their great empire, Jews and Muslims lived and prospered together.

When the Mongol Tartar converted to Islam after capturing Baghdad, he wanted to free all fellow Muslims who had become prisoners. The Muslim scholar Ibn Tammiiya insisted that the King, if he was a true Muslim, must free all non-Muslim prisoners as well, which he did.

CHRISTIANS WERE NOT PERSECUTED by Muslims either, as is evidenced in the historical accounts of the interaction between the two religions during the lifetime of Muhammad. He allowed a Christian delegation from Nejram to stay and even pray in the mosque of the city. It was Prophet Muhammad who advised the Muslims to emigrate to what was then Christian Abyssinia that they might enjoy the justice of the Christian Monarch. It was Muhammad who freed the daughter of Hatem, the ruler of the Christian tribe Tayyi.

As stated previously, many wars and hostile acts did indeed occur between what was essentially the Roman Catholic Church and Islam, especially during the middle ages when individual religious leaders vied for power and domination. Rome and Persia not only rejected Islam and Muhammad as a Prophet of God, but they declared war against Islam. The "war" against Islam on behalf of all Christendom was sanctioned by the Church of Rome. In fact, orders had been given to present the severed head of Muhammad to the Royal Court in Rome, as had been done to many Christians previously. It is a sad reality that even now, as we approach the twenty-first century, men continue to carry out war and acts of aggression in the name of their religions, which in many instances, have become indistinguishable from nationalism.

The original intent of the Message and the Messenger of Islam was to proclaim an invitation to unity, that Jews and Christians might join together with Muslims in the common worship and obedience to the One God of all men and nations. Although this invitation went unanswered, Islam and the Quran do not condemn or persecute them.

"Those who believe in the Quran, and those who follow the Jewish Scriptures, and the Christians and the Sabians, any

who believe in Allah and the Last Day and work righteousness
shall have their reward." (Surah 2:62)

IS GOD THE SAME IN BOTH
THE QURAN AND THE BIBLE?

IN CHAPTER THREE we discussed at some length the nature
and attributes of God as recorded in the Quran. The reader
will recall the centrality of the doctrine of "Tawhid" or unity
of God. To the Muslim, belief in and submission to the One
and only God of the universe is the message of the Quran.
Some of the primary concepts of God in the Quran which
appear nearly identical to those concepts recorded in the
Bible include:

A. ETERNALITY OF GOD... both religions teach that God is
without beginning and without end; God is not bound by the
laws of nature which He created and sustains; He is not a
formed body, nor a measurable substance. The Quran and
the Bible agree that "In the Beginning Was God!" It was God
who began the beginning; it was God, the un-caused cause
that began the eternal observable chain of Cause and Effect,
proving that from nothing, something began to exist, called
into existence by the power of God. To ascribe such power
and absolutes to any other is to practice idolatry or "shirk"
which is considered the unpardonable sin in Islam.

"Allah will not forgive idolatry. He will forgive whom He
will all other sins. He that serves gods beside Allah has strayed
far from the truth." (Surah 4:48)

The Bible likewise condemns the worship of any other
besides Jehovah God as idolatry in the first commandment:

"You shall have no other gods before me. You shall not make
for yourself an idol in the form of anything in heaven above or

*on the earth beneath or in the waters below. You shall not bow
down to them or worship them, for I, the Lord your God am a
jealous God..." (Exodus 20:4, 5)*

A tenacious monotheism accounts for the success of Islam
resisting such human ideologies as communism and capital-
ism, nationalism and materialism. If the citizens of the western nations understood even this one simple, single concept
of Islam, none would have believed the propaganda of governments when they proclaimed various Muslim countries
and leaders as communists. A Muslim can no more be a "card
carrying communist" than a Christian can belong to and support the creed of world atheism.

B. CREATOR... The God of the Quran and the Bible is
acknowledged as the sole creator of all things. Neither
Christian or Muslim believe the universe, the heavens, the
earth and life in all its highly specialized and intricate forms
can be accounted for through "chance probability," or
"random natural selection." Both assign the act of creation
to God:

> *"Your Guardian Lord is Allah, who created the heavens and
> the earth in six days, then He established Himself on the
> Throne of authority. He draws the night as a veil over the day,
> each seek the other in rapid succession; He created the sun, the
> moon, and the stars, all governed by laws under His com-
> mand. Is it not His to create and to govern? Blessed be Allah,
> the Cherisher and Sustainor of the world." (Surah 7:54)*

Every Christian knows the Genesis account of the Bible
which states the very same teaching, that God is the author,
creator and sustainor of all that exists:

"In the beginning God created the heavens and the earth...
God said, "Let there be light," and there was light... He sepa-
rated the light from the darkness. God called the light "day"
and the darkness he called "night." (Genesis 1:1, 3-5)

Both accounts credit God with creating man, but the
Muslim rejects the anthropomorphic suggestion that man is
"made in the image of God." But even here we will find no
disagreement, for the Genesis account does not teach that
God created us to reflect His actual being, for we know that
God is a Spirit, not susceptible to the machinations and frail-
ties of the flesh. We are reflections of God in the gifts of volition or will, intellect, and emotion.

God in both the Quran and the Bible is omnipotent, omniscient and omnipresent. He is the un-created Creator, the
Sovereign Ruler ruling, and the unparalleled Lord of All that
was, is, and shall be.

C. SOVEREIGNTY OF GOD... Islam teaches that God is in
absolute control of all things, including the destiny of
mankind, collectively and individually as well. Allah carries
out His will and way among His creatures and His creation;
nothing occurs without His permission and His Authority.

"With Him are the keys of the unseen, the treasures that no
one knows but He. He knows whatever there is on the earth and
in the sea. Not a leaf falls without His knowledge." (Surah 6:59)

Now compare this concise illustration of God's sovereignty with this scripture in the New Testament encouraging
the disciples of Jesus not to fear men or be concerned for their
daily provisions as they are sent out to preach:

"Are not two sparrows sold for a penny? Yet not one of them
will fall to the ground apart from the will of God. And even the

hairs of your head are numbered. So don't be afraid; you are worth more than many sparrows." (Matthew 10:29-31)

The sovereignty of God in both the Quran and the Bible is remarkably similar. The Old Testament Prophets speak of the Throne of God extending throughout the earth; the God of the Bible causes kings, leaders, and servants to be born to carry out His divine plan as evidenced by Cyrus, King of Persia and many others. And once again in the Quran:

"Allah! there is no god but He; the Living, the Selfsubsisting, Eternal. No slumber or sleep can seize Him; His are all things in the heavens and on the earth... His throne extends over the heavens and the earth..." (Surah 2:255)

Like the Bible, the Quran credits God with rule and reign over all the world, all the nations and empires from the beginning until the end of time! He is forever in control of history, time, and space.

FREEDOM OF CHOICE is not abrogated by the sovereignty of God in Islam or Christianity. Islam's emphasis on the sovereignty of God is often called Fatalism which is incorrect. The sovereignty of God has nothing to do with "fate" or "chance." Acknowledging that God knows all things before they occur, and that the road which each man is destined to travel is already chartered and recorded by God, in no way precludes the moral responsibility of individual choice. God knows the choices we will make and our ultimate destiny, but we do not! Therefore, life is indeed a series of choices based upon our own free will. Whether it is called determinism, predestination, or Calvanism, man will choose his own avenue of life, and God will have laid the pavement for that road or avenue long before our birth.

"In the name of Allah the Compassionate, the Merciful.
Praise be to Allah, the Lord of Creation, the Compassionate,
the Merciful, King of Judgment Day! You alone do we wor-
ship, and to you alone we pray for help. Guide us in the
straight path, the Path of those whom you have favored, not of
those who have incurred your wrath, nor of those gone
astray." (Surah 1:1-7)

Basic differences arise between Islam and Christianity
in the application and understanding of the relationship of
God to mankind. For example, God is never referred to as
"Father" in Islam, for this attributes human characteristics to
the Creator. God has no wife and therefore, human beings are
not the "children of God." Other popular Christian anthro-
pomorphisms including "loving Father," resting on the
Sabbath, hating His enemies, having face, hands, or feet are
viewed suspiciously by Muslims.

Islam likewise rejects the reference to God as "Father of a
nation." Islam rejects the claim by Jews and some Christian
denominations that being born into a Jewish family rather
than obedience and submission to God determines one's
relationship with God.

Indeed, the universality of believers in the One God, along
with numerous biblical passages make clear that the God of
the Bible bears no special allegiance or commitment to any
nation or state today. Believers in God transcend the checker-
board of political systems and human ideologies, and those
who submit to and obey the teachings of God, regardless of
where they are found throughout the world are, in reality,
spiritually related and thus become the only "nation," a spiritual nation of the Holy One.

WHAT DO MUSLIMS REALLY
BELIEVE ABOUT JESUS CHRIST?

JESUS (Isa in Arabic) is referred to by name more than thirty-five times in the Quran, with many other texts containing other titles and names applied to Jesus. As a Christian, I was taught that Muslims reject Jesus Christ, His message, even His historical existence. In the year 1987 in Damascus Syria I was engaged in a marathon dialogue with Grand Mufti, Sheikh Ahmad Kuftaro, the spiritual leader of the Muslims of Syria. As we entered the fifth hour of conversation, the subject shifted to Jesus Christ. Much to my utter surprise, my distinguished host began his opening statement by saying:

"My dear brother, you cannot be a true Muslim unless you love, respect, and honor Jesus."

The Quran refers to Jesus as Messiah, Servant, Son of Mary, Word of God, and Messenger. Even Jesus Himself is considered a revelation from God, and every mention of His name is followed by P.B.U.H., meaning Peace Be Upon Him. In our search for common ground, we will examine the most important teachings of the Quran concerning Jesus Christ. I ask the reader to compare the Quranic text and teachings with that of the New Testament.

A. THE VIRGIN BIRTH OF JESUS begins with the story of Zakariya, the same Zechariah in the narrative of Luke the physician and author of the fourth Gospel. In both books, Zakariya is an aged priest, pleading with God to give him a son, and in both accounts God promises him a son, and in both accounts Zakariya is unable to speak as a sign from God. That son, in both books, is named Yahya or John, meaning life, who became known as the forerunner of Jesus and received the title of "John the Baptizer or Baptist." This entire story is found in Surah's 3 and 19. Notice the strong similarity between the following two texts:

> "His prayer was answered: 'O Zakariya, We give you good news of a son; his name shall be Yahya"(John) (Surah 19:7)

> "Do not be afraid Zechariah; your prayer has been heard. Your wife Elizabeth will bear you a son, and you are to give him the name John." (Luke 1:13)

Nearly forty-five verses of Surah nineteen are devoted to the story of Mary and Jesus. Surah three is a shortened version of Surah nineteen. Compare the following texts from both books depicting the Annunciation to Mary:

> "She said: How shall I have a son, seeing that no man has touched me, and I am chaste (a virgin). The angel replied, "Even so, Allah creates what He wills; When He has decreed a plan, He only says to it 'Be and it is.'" (Surah 3:47)

> "How will this be," Mary asked the angel, "since I am a virgin? The angel answered, "The Holy Sprit will come upon you, and the power of the Most High will overshadow you..." (Luke 1:34,35)

> "Behold the angels said: 'O Mary! Allah gives you glad tidings of a Word from Him: his name Will be Christ Jesus. The son of Mary, held in honor in this world and the hereafter and of the company of those nearest to Allah.'" (Surah 3:45)

> "Do not be afraid, Mary, for you have found favor with God. you will be with child and give birth to a son, and you are to give him the name Jesus. He will be great and will be called

the Son of the Most High. The Lord God will give him the throne of his father David…" (Luke 1:30-32)

Mary, the mother of Jesus is the only woman in the Quran called by her proper name, suggesting the very high regard Muslims have for her, although their regard does not evolve into any manner or form of veneration or worship. Mary is known in the Arabic and Quran as Maryam.

B. JESUS WORKED MIRACLES which are recorded in the Quran, although the list of miracles in the Quran is limited when compared to those in the Injil or New Testament.

> *"Appoint him a messenger to the Children of Israel, with this message: 'I have come to you with a sign from your Lord, in that I make for you out of clay, as it were, the figure of a bird, and breathe into it and it becomes a bird. By Allah's leave I heal those born blind, and the lepers, and I quicken (raise) the dead." (Surah 3:49-51)*

C. THE GOSPEL MESSAGE OF JESUS WAS AUTHENTIC and those to whom Jesus proclaimed the gospel were responsible to adhere to its teachings.

> *"And in their footsteps (the Prophets) we sent Jesus the son of Mary confirming the Law that had come before him: We sent him the Gospel and therein was guidance and light, and confirmation of the Law that had come before him; a guidance and an admonition to those who fear Allah. Let the People of the Gospel judge by what Allah has revealed therein. If any fail to judge by the light of what Allah has revealed, they are no better than those that rebel." (Surah 5:46,47)*

The respected Islamic scholar and translator Abdullah Yusuf Ali comments that the emphasis upon understanding and following "what Allah has revealed" means the message brought by Jesus along with that proclaimed by Muhammad. It is such statements which cause Muslims to hold Jesus in such high esteem, and sense a kinship with true Christian believers, as reflected in the following texts:

> *"Nearest among them in love to the believers you will find those who say 'We are Christians;' because among these are men devoted to learning and men who have renounced the world, and they are not arrogant." (Surah 5:82)*

> *"Not all of them are alike; of the People of the Book are a portion that stand for the right; they rehearse the signs of Allah all night long, and they prostrate themselves in adoration. They believe in Allah and the Last Day; they enjoin what is right, and forbid what is wrong; and they hasten in emulation in all good works; they are in the ranks of the righteous. Of the good that they do, nothing will be rejected of them; for Allah knows well those who do right." (Surah 3:113-115)*

D. THE RESURRECTION OF JESUS is considered the bedrock of Christianity. To the Muslim, Jesus was "raised" by God in some fashion perhaps similar to Enoch when he was "taken up" or translated. The Quran foretells the raising of Jesus in the following text:

> *"Behold! Allah said: 'O Jesus! I will take you, and raise you to Myself and clear you of the falsehoods of those who blaspheme; I will make those who follow you superior to those who reject faith' to the day of Resurrection: then shall you all return to me, and I will judge between you of the matters of dispute." (Surah 3:55)*

A clear reference to the resurrection of Jesus Christ is found in the following text attributed to Jesus which seems to be predictive prophecy:

"So Peace is upon me the day I was born, the day that I die, and the Day that I shall be raised up to life again." (Surah 19:33)

DO MUSLIMS BELIEVE IN THE CRUCIFIXION OF JESUS?

THE CRUCIFIXION OF JESUS CHRIST is not accepted as fact by Islam and the Quran. Indeed, the Quran clearly states that, although the Jews claimed to have crucified Jesus, they did not crucify him, but either through trickery or some manner of deception, substituted someone else on the cross instead of Jesus. Denial of the crucifixion, along with the clear rejection of any claims of Jesus in the Gospel record of being the Incarnation of God and given all authority in both heaven and earth, represent the single greatest difference between Islam and Christianity. The rejection of the crucifixion and deity of Christ is not surprising when considering the concept of "Tawhid" or unity of God.

To the Muslim, it is beyond comprehension to believe that the God of the universe came to the earth in human form, born of a woman, raised in obscurity, retaining all His authority and power, while at the same time permitting evil men to carry out their plan to execute Him by crucifixion on a tree between two common thieves. God has no equal, nor does he marry or produce offspring, thus the "Sonship" along with the crucifixion of Jesus are assumed to be later "additions" to Christian faith and doctrine.

"(The Jews) boast, 'we killed Christ Jesus the son of Mary, the Messenger of Allah' but they killed him not, nor crucified him. But it was made to appear so to them… No, Allah raised him up to Himself, and Allah is exalted in Power." (Surah 4:157,158)

But what does this text teach concerning the resurrection of Jesus? Does it imply a physical death but a living spirit? Or did Jesus only "appear to die" as numerous "higher critics" of the Bible have long contended? Was a last minute substitute who closely resembled Jesus nailed to the cross instead? To the Christian, in light of the science of Textual Criticism, using such methodologies as hermeneutics, historicity, and cannonicity in considering the New Testament text, the answer is a resounding NO! To the Christian, the focus of faith is upon the PERSON of Jesus, whereas, to the Muslim, the focus of faith is upon the MESSAGE of Jesus. To the Muslim, it is difficult to reconcile the crucifixion of Jesus Christ with the justice, mercy, power and wisdom of God. If God could and did forgive Adam and Eve their original sin, would He need to supply a sacrifice for the rest of mankind? Basically, most Muslims believe that Jesus was saved from death by being raised or resurrected by the power of God. Either before his physical death or while still living, an ascension took place, and Jesus Christ was raised to be with God.

WHAT OTHER BIBLICAL SUBJECTS
DOES THE QURAN ADDRESS?

Christians are quite surprised to learn of the extensive list of biblical subjects considered vital to the Christian faith which are likewise important to the Muslim faith. The Quran has much to say regarding many of the pertinent theological and doctrinal subjects of Christianity, but since this book is not intended as an exhaustive commentary on Islam, we will consider only a few of the more familiar and important subjects considered basic to the Christian faith.

A. ANGELS... (Malaik) The reader will recall that belief in the existence of angels is one of the five primary elements of Islamic faith which falls under the heading of Shahadah. The

Quran teaches that angels are spiritual beings who do the will of God; they require no food, drink, or sleep; they possess no physical or material desires or needs. Their number is innumerable, and each one has a specific duty. Angels were created by God to minister to the needs of mankind. Muslims consider Gabriel to be the most important angel as evidenced by his message to Mary and, they believe, his appearance to Muhammad. The Quran teaches that we really do have "guardian angels" sent to protect us throughout our lives.

> *"We are your protectors in this life and in the hereafter."*
> *(Surah 41:31)*

Even from the time of our birth, every person is assigned two angels, the first to keep a record of the good deeds during our lifetime, and the second to record the evil or bad deeds. God in His omniscience is fully aware of all of our deeds and actions, but the recording by the angels is intended to encourage man to good deeds and to assure us that absolute justice will be forthcoming from God when all men stand before Him in the final Day of Judgement.

Angels accompany us throughout the journey of life and into eternity where they stand with us before the Throne of Judgement where we will account for our deeds before God.

> *"But verily over you are appointed angles to protect you...*
> *kind and honourable, writing down your deeds. They know*
> *and understand all that you do." (Surah 82:10-12)*

Faithful and obedient believers in God are assured that in times of hardship and oppression, angels will give us the courage necessary to withstand and overcome.

> *"In the case of those who say, "Our Lord is Allah," and fur-*
> *ther, stand straight and steadfast, the angels descend on them*

from time to time: "Fear not and do not grieve, but receive the
glad tidings of the garden of bliss that you were promised."
(Surah 41:30)

Believers are reminded to focus upon the promised reward
of eternal life and happiness in the "garden" or heaven. The
Christian readily understands these portrayals of angels in
the Quran, since angels are an integral part of Christianity
and are credited with seeming identical powers and purpose
in both the Old and New Testaments. It was the "angel of
God" who came to Hagar and her young son in the barren
wilderness, causing a well to appear and save them from
dying of thirst, and then promising, on behalf of God, that
the young boy would be the progenitor of a great nation.

> *"And God heard the lad crying, and the angel of God called*
> *to Hagar from heaven, and said to her, 'What is the matter with*
> *you Hagar? Do not fear, for God has heard the voice of the lad*
> *where he is. Arise, lift up the lad, and hold him by the hand; for*
> *I will make a great nation of him.'" (Genesis 21:17,18)*

Gabriel and Michael are two prominent angels who are
given numerous missions in both the testaments, and Gabriel
is considered the more prominent of all angels in both the
Quran and the Bible. It was Gabriel, whose name means
"man of God" in the hebrew, who delivered the messages to
Hagar, Daniel, Mary, and Zachariah, and it was Gabriel who
delivered the Quran to Prophet Muhammad.

B. HEAVEN, HELL AND ETERNITY... In his famous "Dante's
Inferno" Dante borrowed heavily from Islamic poets to offer
a description of the terrors of hell. Indeed, the Quran por-
trays in vivid detail the suffering that awaits those who
choose to live their lives indifferent to the realities of the

existence of God and His revelation to mankind. Like Christianity and the Bible, the Quran depicts a place of reward for the faithful, and a place of punishment for the disobedient. The metaphor "garden" is the place of reward, the "heaven" of the Muslim believer. After standing judgement before God, the faithful arrive at the Garden of Bliss where they will enjoy flowing streams, a permanent oasis, rivers of milk that never sour, fountains of honey, luscious fruit of every kind.

> "Say: 'Shall I give you Glad tidings of things far better than those? For the righteous are Gardens in nearness to their Lord, with rivers flowing beneath; there is their eternal home; with companions pure and holy and the good pleasure of Allah.'" (Surah 3:15)

> "Here is a Parable of the Garden which the righteous are promised: In it are rivers of water incorruptible, rivers of milk of which the taste never changes; and rivers of wine, a joy to those who drink; and rivers of honey pure and clear. In it are all kinds of fruit; and grace from their Lord." (Surah 47:15)

Please notice this image of heaven is referred to in Surah 47:15 as a parable, which comes to us from the Greek word "parabolis" which, according to Webster's Collegiate Dictionary, means "a fictitious story that illustrates a moral attitude or a religious principle." The description of heaven in the Christian Bible is likewise parabolic in nature, as the following text illustrates:

> "Bring the whole tithe into the storehouse, so that there may be food in My house, and test Me now in this says the Lord of hosts, if I will not open for you the windows of heaven and

pour out for you a blessing until there is no more need."
(Malachi 3:10)

The book of Revelation in the New Testament makes full use of numerous images and parables to illustrate heaven. Heaven is said to have doors, thrones, stars, angels coming down to earth, and a multitude of other descriptive terms. Most of these are found in the book of Revelation, where heaven is depicted as a place where "there shall no longer be any death, no longer any mourning, or crying, or pain." (Revelation 21). Now compare the Quranic parables cited with the following:

"And he showed me a river of the water of life, clear as crystal, coming from the throne of God and of the Lamb, in the middle of its street. And on either side of the river was the tree of life, bearing twelve kinds of fruit, yielding its fruit every month; and the leaves of the tree were for the healing of nations." (Revelation 22:1, 2)

Christians have long imagined heaven to be their eternal resting place or abode, with "streets paved with gold and precious stones," etc. When we consider the historical and cultural background when both the Quran and the Bible were written, we then understand the usage of word imagery to describe heaven to the earliest followers. Both attempt to draw a picture of a world beyond sense perception in the terms of the world we see, feel, and experience.

HELL IS PORTRAYED by both the Quran and the Bible as a final abode for the wicked, the unrighteous, the immoral and the skeptic. Both describe hell as a continual punishment, suffering from flame and fire and other manner of pain and torment.

"One day the earth will be changed to a different earth and so will be the heavens, and men will be marshalled forth, before Allah, the One, the Irresistible; and you will see the sinners that day, bound together in fetters… their garments of liquid pitch, and their faces covered with fire." (Surah 14:48,49)

"For the rejectors (of God) we have prepared chains, yokes, and a blazing fire." (Surah 76:4)

"And if your eye causes you to stumble, cast it out; it is better for you to enter the kingdom of God with one eye, than having two eyes, to be cast into hell where their worm does not die, and the fire is not quenched. For everyone will be salted with fire." (Mark 9:47-49)

"The Son of Man will send forth His angels, and they will gather out of His kingdom all stumbling blocks, and those who commit lawlessness, and will cast them into the furnace of fire; in that place there shall be weeping and gnashing of teeth." (Matthew 13:41,42)

Among Muslims as well as Christians, there are those who view the statements of the Garden (Heaven) and the Fire (Hell) as quite literal. Still others consider the promised joys of heaven and the punishments of hell to be symbolic or spiritual. But in neither religion are they to be considered the proverbial "carrot and stick" and motivation or reason for obedience and service to God. To both Muslim and Christian, striving to be morally responsible and seeking to uphold the virtues of Justice, Mercy, and Compassion in this life will indeed prepare us for the life to come.

C. JUDGEMENT DAY… A third common belief between Muslim and Christian. A final day of judgement or reckoning is closely allied with the resurrection. Islam teaches that all of humanity will be raised from the dead and all will likewise stand before God to receive His judgement. This final act is referred to in the Quran as the Day of Retribution, Day of Wrath, Day of Decision, Day of Truth, and Day of Muster. On this day, the deeds of every man will be weighed by God and rewarded accordingly; the righteous will enter the Garden of Bliss, and the wicked, the Fire:

"As for the righteous, they will be in Bliss; and the wicked, they will be in the Fire which they will enter on the day of Judgement, and they will not be able to keep away therefrom." (Surah 82:13-16)

The Quran states that the Day of Judgement will be preceded by times of chaos, turbulence and unnatural phenomena affecting all of creation and nature. Strong parallels can be seen between the occurrences at the time of Judgement in Islam and the second and final return of Jesus Christ in the Bible. Both accounts make clear that these events are the climactic conclusions of the world and all humanity. When these events take place, eternity begins.

"When the sky is torn asunder, when the stars are scattered, when the oceans are caused to burst forth, and when the graves are turned upside down, then shall each soul know what it has given and what it has kept back." (Surah 82:1-5)

"But immediately after the tribulation of those days the sun will be darkened, and the moon will not give its light, and the stars will fall from the sky, and the powers of the heavens will be shaken, and then the sign of the Son of Man will appear in the sky, and then all the tribes of the earth will mourn, and they will see the Son of Man coming on the clouds of the sky with power and great glory." (Matthew 24:29,30)

The Day of Judgement, to both Christian and Muslim, will be an accounting, where each person must answer for his own actions and deeds while on this earth.

> *"On that day of Judgement we shall confront him with a book spread wide open, saying, Here is your book; read it. Enough for you this day that your own soul shall call you to account." (Surah 17:13-14)*

> *"The sins of men are quite evident, going before them to the judgement; for others, their sins follow after. Likewise also, deeds that are good are quite evident, and those which are otherwise cannot be concealed." (I Timothy 5:24,25)*

In Islam, the believer will be confronted by even the slightest deeds of good and evil committed during his sojourn on earth. All disputes, all issues of truth and justice will be decided and clarified by the Final Arbiter who is the "witness to all things." (Surah 22:17)

THE BIBLE teaches that the return of Christ will precede the resurrection and final judgement, and even the Quran points to Jesus as a sign for the coming "Hour of Judgement." As we have noted in our study of Jesus earlier in this chapter, Islam teaches that Jesus will have a vital role to play in the consummation of the ages.

> *"And Jesus shall be a Sign for the coming of the Hour of Judgement. Therefore have no doubt about the Hour, but follow me; this is a straight way."(Surah 43:61)*

> *"And there is none of the People of the Book but must believe in him before his death; and on the Day of Judgement He will be a witness against them." (Surah 4:159)*

For both Christian and Muslim, the Judgement of God awaits all mankind; all will account for the acts, thoughts and deeds of a lifetime. For both Christian and Muslim, the questions are the same; will our deeds and actions committed and omitted during our lifetimes reflect the faith we avowed? Will our good deeds outweigh the bad? One thing is certain, the Judgement of God will be swift, it will be fair, and it will be final.

D. The origin and concept of sin... is at once similar yet distinct from the biblical account in that man is a free moral agent capable of choosing to do right or wrong, obedience or disobedience to God's commands, yet born into this life without original sin! Islam teaches that man can no more be born with original sin than he can be born an original saint. The Quran sets forth the position that all are born innocent, pure, true, free, and disposed towards worshipping God and doing good. This is called "fitrah." Since man is created by God and infused with His spirit, it is a natural conclusion that man will enter this world in an absolute attitude of innocence. To the Muslim, sin is not what we are, but rather what we do. Sin is a consequence of influence from a wayward world and society; a byproduct of disdain and departure from the revelation of Allah. Sin, like eternal reward, cannot be hereditary or inherited, but must be achieved by deliberate acts of the individual.

> "Behold! The Lord said to the angels, I am about to create man, from sounding clay, from mud moulded into shape; When I have fashioned him and breathed into him my spirit, fall down in obesiance to him." (Surah 15:28,29)

The "breath" or "spirit" of God within us precludes every human being from coming into this life a sinner. Man is a strange combination of egoism and altruism; he is not born inclined to do good or evil, but has the potential and the choice to do both. The Muslim scholar U.A. Samad in "A Comparative Study of Christianity and Islam" states:

> "To say that a man is sinful even before he has committed a sin and that every child is born with a depraved nature, inherently and utterly incapable of avoiding sin would be an aspersion upon the Creator." (pages 95, 96)

In Islam, a sin is any act, thought, or will that is (1) deliberate, (2) defies the unequivocal law of God, (3) violates the right of God or the right of man, (4) is harmful to the soul or body, (5) is committed repeatedly and is (6) normally avoidable. In summary, sin is the forgetting of God, a deliberate conscious violation of God's Will or Revelation.

E. REPENTANCE AND FORGIVENESS for sins is part and parcel of the Islamic faith. Repentance must come first before forgiveness, and both must be sincerely demonstrated if one is to enter eternal Bliss or Heaven.

> "And O my people! Ask forgiveness of your Lord, then turn to Him in repentance; He will cause the sky to rain abundance on you and will add strength to your strength. So do not turn back to sin." (Surah 11:52)

In the arid desert country of Arabia, rain was one of the greatest blessings God could bestow upon His people. Thus, when the Quran spoke of abundant rain being a parallel with abundant forgiveness, they understood the application to forgiveness of sin as reflecting the mercy and compassion of God. He is forgiving and reassuring to the sinner who repents and who does not return to repeat that sin.

*"Seek forgiveness from your Lord then turn towards Him;
My Lord is Merciful, and Affectionate." (Surah 11:90)*

ONE SIN IS WORSE THAN all others, and that is the worship
or equation of any other person, place or thing with the
Majesty of God. Called "shirk" in Arabic, this sin is considered
the most grevious.

*"God does not forgive anyone for associating something
with Him; He forgives whomever He wishes for anything
besides that. Anyone who gives God associates has indeed
invented an awful offence." (Surah 4:46)*

The many Surahs which address shirk indicate the importance
and magnitude of this sin. Taken as a whole, the Quran
teaches that no truly submitted follower of Allah can allow
anyone or anything to attain the same level of sacredness and
devotion as the One True God of the universe. Anyone who
does so has obviously fallen far from God and would not
seek forgiveness from Him. However, if the polytheist or
atheist is repentant and seeks forgiveness and returns to the
worship of God alone, they too can be forgiven.

In conclusion, Islam teaches that relatively speaking,
humans are good, radically free, and capable of change. Sin is
not inescapable but avoidable and not inevitable. To sin
requires a deliberate decision to violate the unequivocal law
of God. Rather than a "fall from grace," Islam teaches man
descends from the higher level upon which he arrives in this
world to the lower levels of spiritual deterioration and alienation
from God through willful acts of disobedience. These
acts are, collectively, called sin.

Chapter Five
Popular Distortions and Misconceptions of Islam

In the earlier periods of history, Christianity was a new and hated religion. Those who called themselves Christians were belittled, abused, even arrested and executed solely because they proclaimed themselves and their religion to be from God. Dislike and disdain accompanied nearly every Christian throughout the Roman empire; false charges and accusations, including the misrepresentation of the teachings of the Bible, were commonplace, and political rulers used all manner of false and malicious propaganda to foment hate and distrust between their citizens and the adherents of the new religion called Christianity.

Today, similar attacks, including the use of the same propaganda methods used to assail Christianity from its earliest inception, are being utilized to attack and discredit the great religion of Islam. Daily attacks appear in both the print and electronic media of the Western nations, and after years of such attacks, great walls and barriers now separate not only Christians from Muslims, but fact from fiction, truth from lies, and therefore, peace from war, tolerance from intolerance.

The mass media have centered their reporting on the more menacing and extreme aspects of Islam creating, sustaining, and promoting the false image of Islam as a violent, xenophobic, aggressive, fanatical and fatalistic religion. This artificial, stereotyped image is presented in serious books and articles, as well as popular films and literature. The Muslim has become the modern day "whipping boy" for secular politicians as well as the "God-haters" of the world. Sadly, millions of Christians have accepted the distortions and propaganda as fact without the slightest knowledge of the tenets and teachings of Islam, which is one of the primary purposes of this book. This author has spent a considerable amount of his life living, studying, and working with and among the Muslim populations of the world. Having firsthand knowledge of the true nature of Islam and the Muslim people in Jerusalem, Egypt, Lebanon and Syria in the Middle East, and of India, Pakistan and Kashmir in Asia, and of Great Britain, France, Canada and the United States in the western hemisphere, I can authoritatively attest to the true nature and disposition of the majority of Muslims in the world today.

The majority of Muslims world-wide believe their faith means carrying out the will of God in their daily lives, a life of religious commitment nourished by means of prayer and fasting; by reading, reciting and meditating upon the words of the Holy Quran. To the true Muslim, family life is of primary importance. Central values revolve around honesty in business, hospitality and cordiality, sexual purity and morality, pardoning others who offend them, and generosity towards the poor. The Islamic ideal, from the very beginning in Mecca and for the greater number of Muslims today, is that of a quiet, simple, upright, and God-fearing life.

It is not my intent to glorify Muslims for they, like Christians, Jews, Buddhists and all other religions have their share of charlatans, impostors, pretenders, and self-appointed spokesmen. But if Muslims and the religion of Islam are to be judged by the actions and policies of a miniscule few who preach violence, hatred and death, then Christians and Christianity, Jews and Judaism, Buddhists and Buddhism, all must likewise be judged by those exact same standards.

If the human rights in some Muslim countries are not respected, they must be judged alongside the human rights in "Christian" countries like Guatemala, Chile, El Salvador and the Philippines, and the "orthodox" Serbs of the former

Yugoslavia. Distorted and negative perceptions of the religion of Islam owe their origin to outright false accusations and half truths. In this chapter we will examine some of the most widely known and oft-repeated accusations against the religion of Islam. These accusations represent the most frequently asked questions I have received during the many years of lectures and seminars on Islam.

DOESN'T ISLAM TREAT WOMEN AS POSSESSIONS, AND AREN'T THEY OPPRESSED AND DISCRIMINATED AGAINST?

First of all, we must draw the distinction between what the Quran and therefore Islam teaches, and the actions and attitudes of chauvinistic, male-dominated tribal cultures. The treatment of women in some Gulf States as well as a few African and Asian countries is more the result of a strong patriarchal tradition coupled with the most conservative INTERPRETATION of Islamic law rather than adherence to the teachings of the Quran. Indeed, in the Hadith it is recorded that the Prophet Muhammad himself once said:

> *"Paradise lies at the feet of mothers. All human beings (male and female) are equal, equal as the teeth of a comb. There is no superiority of a white over a black nor of any male over the female. Only the God-consciousness (regardless of gender) merit favor and the ultimate rewards from God."*

The popular, well-known negative aspects of how women are treated in particular Islamic States or countries must be viewed in the context of cultural traditions. When we consider the status of women in the pre-Islamic societies we learn that two-thirds were in some form of slavery. Sadly, women have been the object of discrimination and disrespect for most of the generations of mankind. They had no personal rights, no legal or social status. In point of fact, female infanticide was a common practice. Men throughout history dominated women as an inferior and weaker sex, incapable of self-sufficiency, utterly helpless without the provision and protection of a husband. Before Islam, women were nearly invisible in a male-dominated world in nearly every religion and every culture of the world. Numerous examples can be found in the Encyclopedia Brittanica of 1911. What was the status of women in the Hindu religion and culture?

> *"In India, subjection was a cardinal principle. Day and night must women be held by their protectors in a state of dependence, says Manu. A good wife is a woman whose mind, speech and body are kept in subjection, acquires high renown in this world, and, in the next, the same abode with her husband." (pg 782)*

THE ROMAN EMPIRE, which many credit with bringing law and advanced forms of government and civility to European and Western nations, practiced rank discrimination against women as evidenced in "History of Civilization" by E. Allen:

> *"A Roman wife was described by historians as a babe, a minor, a ward, a person incapable of doing or acting anything according to her own individual taste, a person continually under the tutelage and guardianship of her husband." (pg 550)*

Once again, in the Encyclopedia Brittanica, 11th edition, we have a summation of Roman Law regarding women:

> *"In Roman Law a woman was even in historic times completely dependent. If married she and her property passed into*

the power of her husband… the wife was the purchased property of her husband, and like a slave acquired only for his benefit. A woman could not exercise any civil or public office; could not be a witness, surety, tutor, or curator; she could not adopt or be adopted, or make will or contract." (page 783)

The women of ancient Greece fared no better despite the "advanced civilization" and the "golden age" of some of the greatest philosophers and thinkers of all time. Athenian women were viewed as helpless children, forever in need of guidance, protection, and provision from male benefactors.

"Athenian women were always minors, subject to some male; to their father, to their brother, or to some other male kin. Her consent in marriage was generally thought unnecessary and she was obliged to submit to the wishes of her parents, and receive from them her husband and her lord, even though he were a stranger to her." (E.Allen, History of Civilization, pg 443-444)

The greatest Hellenic philosophers declared that the state would become radically disorganized if women were given equal status with their husbands. Aristotle considered women to be "inferior beings." Demosthenes and Plato suggested women live together in a totally separate "community of wives." The historical period of the Old Testament bore witness to a changing view towards women, as under the Hebrew system, women gained greater personal liberties, including social and economic equality. Sarah, the wife of Abraham, the spiritual "father" of Christians, Muslims and Jews, held a position of favor and authority. Rachel won from Jacob a love that accepted her as an equal in the companionship and counsels of family life. Many hebrew women rose to positions of prominence and national leadership such as Miriam, the sister of Aaron and Moses who led the massive celebration of victory over their enemies in Exodus 15:20.

The prophetess Deborah became the virtual judge of the nation and even led the armies to victory as recorded in the book of Judges, especially Judges 4:8, and no person in all of Israel surpassed Hannah, the mother of Samuel in intelligence, beauty, and religious devotion. (I Samuel 2:1-10) Still, marriage was "arranged" between parents and suitors not necessarily with the consent of the woman. This is clearly the case in the story of Jacob who "made a deal" to work for Laban for seven years in order to "earn" Rachel, one of his two daughters, as his wife. The Biblical text is clear regarding the status and rights of women:

> *"Jacob was in love with Rachel and said, 'I will work for you for seven years in return for your younger daughter Rachel.' Laban said, 'It's better to give her to you than to some other man.'" (Genesis 29:18f)*

The Old Testament pages contain story after story of women being given to men as wives, women servants given as sexual partners and surrogate "birth mothers" such as Hagar who gave birth to Ishmael.

CHRISTIANITY AND THE NEW TESTAMENT brought a marked departure from the old world view of women as chattel and property, to a position of honor, reverence, and nobility. From Mary, the mother of Jesus, to Mary and Martha who opened their home in Bethany to Jesus and the Disciples, the women of the New Testament exemplify the true role of women as wives, devout followers and teachers, worthy of equal recognition and respect. Six hundred years later, Islam likewise brought a new emphasis on the status and freedoms rightly due the women of the world. Now, we will examine what the Quran teaches Muslims and the world concerning the role of women in matters of the Spirit, Society, Economics, and Politics. The reader will be challenged to compare what true Islam teaches with the practices of backward and uneducated, chauvinistic and insecure, male oriented societies and governments.

A. THE SPIRITUAL ASPECT OF WOMEN IN THE QURAN must be understood by beginning at the same point of origin as that found in the Bible, the creation narratives. We have already compared the accounts of both books and religions and noted the strong similarities. But the Quran and Islam differ from the Bible and Christianity in that the Quran does not blame Eve or women for Adam's willful sin and fall in the garden of Eden. Both were jointly wrong in their disobedience to God's instructions, and both repented, and both were forgiven.

> *"Then began Satan to whisper suggestions to them, in order to reveal to them their shame that was hidden from them. He said 'Your Lord only forbade you this tree lest you should become angels or such beings as live forever' So by deceit he brought about their fall: when they tasted of the tree, their shame became known to them, and they began to sew together the leaves of the garden over their bodies." (Surah 7:20-22)*

The first couple created by God were both equally guilty of ignoring the commands and warnings of God and were cast out of the garden. Woman is recognized by Islam as a full and equal partner of man in the procreation of mankind as he being the "father" and she being the "mother" are both essential for life.

"O mankind! We created you from a single pair of a male and a female and made you into Nations and tribes that you may know each other." (Surah 49:13)

Mankind is descended from one pair of parents. Their tribes, races, and nations are convenient labels by which we may know certain differing characteristics but before Allah, they are all one and they, like their original parents, share equally in the rewards for righteousness and punishments for disobedience.

WOMEN RECEIVE THE SAME SPIRITUAL REWARDS as do men believers and have the same access to heaven:

"If any do deeds of righteousness, be they male or female, and they have faith, they will enter Heaven." (Surah 4:124)

"Whoever works righteousness, man or woman, and has faith, to them will we give a new life and life that is good and pure, and we will bestow on such their reward according to the best of their actions." (Surah 16:97)

"For Muslim men and women, for believing men and women, for devout men and women, for true men and women, for men and women who humble themselves, for men and women who give in charity, for men and women who fast and deny themselves, for men and women who guard their chastity, and for men and women who engage in praise of Allah, for them Allah has prepared forgiveness and great reward." (Surah 35:33)

From these brief texts from the Quran it should now be patently clear that the religion of Islam considers women to be the spiritual equal of men; that men are not in any manner "preferred" before God, and that faithful and obedient Muslim women will receive the exact same spiritual rewards in the eternal Garden of Bliss.

B. THE SOCIAL STATUS OF WOMEN in Islam, as clearly revealed in the Quran, is again a position of equality and high esteem. The value of women in Islam is revealed in the Quranic texts which contradicted the prejudicial attitudes and practices against women at the time the Quran was given to Prophet Muhammad in ancient Arabia. A common but terrible activity of many cultures for many centuries was the practice of female infanticide. This despicable act is still practiced in some parts of India, Africa and Asia. Some of the pagan Arabs hated to have daughters since they were in a perpetual state of war and in need of warrior sons to help fight their enemies, thus the murderous act of burying female children quickly became widespread. The low estate of women is depicted in the following text which reveals that a newborn girl and daughter was either killed or even if kept, became a cause for scorn and derision heaped upon the father by other tribes and leaders.

> *"When news is brought to one of them of the birth of a female child, his face darkens, and he is filled with inward grief. With shame he hides himself from his people, because of the bad news he has had. Shall he keep it and suffer contempt, or bury it in the dust? Ah! What an evil choice they decide on."* (Surah 16:58,59)

The Quran reminds these pagans that although the innocent child may have had no voice to oppose its own murder, when the Day of Judgement occurs, she will then testify against her murderer and Justice will prevail.

"When the oceans boil over with a swell; when the souls are sorted out; when the female infant buried alive is questioned for what crime she was killed; then shall each soul know (and be responsible for) the deeds done with his own hands." (Surah 81:6-9, 14)

A well known Hadith of Prophet Muhammad addressed the murder of infant girls and clearly contradicts the practice of favoring a boy over a girl in the same family.

"Whosoever has a daughter and he does not bury her alive, does not insult her, and does not favour his son over her, God will enter him into Paradise. Whosoever supports two daughters till they mature, he and I will come in the day of judgement as this (and he pointed with his two fingers close together). (Ibn Hanbal, No. 1957)

MAJOR DISTORTIONS ABOUND CONCERNING MARRIAGE in the religion of Islam. Women and wives, it is claimed, are considered mere property and servants, denied personal freedoms of choice and even the most basic of human rights. We will consider only a few of the most popular and common accusations and misconceptions about Muslim women and marriage and once again we will permit the Quran and the Sunnah to set forth the intended practice and norm.

"DO MUSLIM WOMEN HAVE A CHOICE IN A MARRIAGE PROPOSAL?"

According to Islamic law called Shariah, which is taken from the Quran and the Sunnah, no Muslim woman can be forced to marry anyone without her personal consent. The fantasy image of a beautiful young maiden being forced to marry a cruel but rich old man, chosen by her parents, is the plot for numerous films made in Hollywood in America. Consider the following Hadith on this important question:

> "*Ibn Abbas reported that a girl came to the Messenger of God, Muhammad (peace be upon him), and she reported that her father had forced her to marry without her consent. The Messenger of God gave her the choice between accepting the marriage or invalidating it.*" (Ibn Hanbal, No. 2469)

In another version of this same occurrence, the girl said:

> "*Actually I accept this marriage but I wanted to let women know that parents have no right to force a husband on them.*" (Ibn Majah, No. 1873)

It is true that according to Islamic teaching, parents should look for the most suitable partner for their children to ensure a happy and lasting marriage, but the final decision still remains with the man and woman. As a young archaeology student living and studying among Muslims in several foreign countries, I have personally witnessed the progressive steps of marriage between two consenting people. THE WOMAN ALWAYS HAS THE RIGHT TO TERMINATE THE RELATION-SHIP! The couple spends time together closely observed by a chaperone, usually a relative of the girl's family. After a lengthy period of what the early Americans called "courting," final plans are made for the wedding. Since all parties realize they are marrying into an entire extended family, both families familiarize themselves with one another, thus eliminating many of the tensions and conflicts commonly associated with "in-laws" in Western society.

The Quran clearly indicates that marriage is for sharing between the two halves of society, and that its objectives, beside perpetuating human life, are emotional well-being and spiritual harmony. Its basic foundation is built upon love and mercy.

> *"And among His Signs is this, that he created spouses for you from among yourselves so that you may console yourselves with them. He has planted love and mercy between you; in that are signs for people who reflect." (Surah 30:21)*

A man and wife are expected to find tranquility in each other's company and be bound together not only by sexual relationship but by "love and mercy." This description of marriage and relationship between man and woman comprises mutual care, consideration, respect and affection. Husbands and wives are referred to as "garments" for each other, providing mutual support, comfort, and protection, fitting each other as a garment fits the body.

> *"(Your wives) are your garments, and you are their garments." (Surah 2:187)*

> *"The most perfect believers are the best in conduct and the best of you are those who are best to their wives." (Muhammad, Hadith Ibn Hanbal, No. 7396)*

Unlike many cultures and religions, Islam does not support the "selling" of a woman into marriage by means of a "dowry" being paid to the parents. In fact, when a woman is married it is an essential part of the marriage for the bridegroom to GIVE HER A DOWRY, called Mahr, which may be any value agreed upon. This is not the same as the African and Asian "bride-price" which is a "compensation" given to the father of the bride. The Muslim dowry is a gift from the bridegroom to the bride and it is her own exclusive property. DIVORCE is to be avoided if at all humanly possible. The Quran suggests every effort be made to reconcile the two persons involved, but if all else fails, the woman has the same right as the man to end the marriage. If divorce occurs, the woman should wait three months, during which time her husband remains responsible for her welfare and maintenance. The purpose of this waiting period is to clarify whether the woman is pregnant, and also serves as a "cooling-off" period providing family members, friends and community leaders an opportunity to attempt reconciliation. During the three months, the husband cannot remove her from the house, but the woman may leave if she so desires.

> "If you fear a breach between a man and his wife, send for an arbiter from his family and an arbiter from her family. If both want to be reconciled, God will adjust things between them." (Surah 4:35)

If the couple is reconciled they may resume the marriage at any time within the three month waiting period, whereupon the divorce is automatically revoked. This can be repeated a second time, but if the threat of divorce occurs a third time the divorce becomes irrevocable.

C. THE ECONOMIC RIGHTS OF WOMEN IN ISLAM are little known to those living in the West, even though these rights and privileges have not changed over the past fourteen hundred years. Can Muslim women own anything separate and apart from their husbands? Can they legally enter in to legal contracts and transactions on their own behalf? Are women permitted to be employed and to work outside the home, and if so, what happens to the salary or money she earns?

INDEPENDENT OWNERSHIP is one of the most fundamental rights of Muslim women. In Islamic law, a woman's right to her own money, land, property and other negotiable assets is indisputably acknowledged and is not subject to change or alteration even by marriage. Whatever wealth she has acquired prior to marriage remains hers alone, to do with as she so desires. Muslim women are free to buy, sell, exchange, mortgage or lease the whole or part of their properties, independent of consultation with their husbands, and without their consent.

ANY PERSONAL INCOME, whether it be gained from profits, rents, capital appreciation or job earnings, belongs entirely to her and cannot be used by anyone else, including her husband, to pay for the normal costs of everyday living. It is the husband's responsibility to provide a home, education and general welfare for his wife and children.

D. ARE MUSLIM WOMEN ALLOWED TO WORK AND APPEAR IN PUBLIC?

THE GULF WAR provided the basis of one of the most popular accusations of gender bias against Islam when American soldiers returned home from the Gulf region giving accounts of women held hostage, not allowed to leave their homes, forbidden to drive automobiles alone, and generally speaking, prohibited from appearing in public.

The Quran contains no text supporting such practices against Muslim women. It is indeed true that some Muslim countries and societies have "rediscovered" and are attempting to implement customs and practices of past centuries regarding the status of women. Truthfully speaking, these archaic attitudes and practices are not universally accepted or applied by Muslims and are observed only by a minority. The influence of Western civilization on the entire world has, in effect, altered and broadened womans' role in society. The changes wrought vary from one Muslim country to another. The impact of modernization (Westernization) on women in middle east countries such as Egypt, Syria, and Lebanon contrasts sharply with that experienced by women in Saudi Arabia and the United Arab Emirates. Indeed, a sharp contrast can be found between urban and rural areas within the same country. Not only are women "permitted" to work outside the home and "appear" in public in many Islamic countries, but the author has personally met and worked with Muslim women holding some of the highest and most important political posts in their respective governments, including Cabinet Ministers, Ambassadors, and Prime Ministers. The author has also worked with numerous Muslim women in the world of academia and jurisprudence, including the heads of Graduate School departments and Supreme Court Judges. I found these extremely capable women no less devout in their faith and practice of Islam then any other Muslim, man or woman. If a woman wishes to work, she is free to do so providing her integrity and honor are secure.

THE QURAN DOES NOT FORBID a woman from accepting employment or pursuing a professional career. It is especially good if she chooses a career which seems more compatible with her distinct nature, aptitude and abilities such as a doctor, nurse, teacher, etc.

The secluding of women is known as "purdah" in the Arabic, and is without any clear text in the Quran. In fact, the Quran speaks clearly of women participating in the life of the community and common religious responsibility with men to worship God, and live virtuous lives. Muslim women in early Islam fought and prayed alongside their men in battle. And the reader will recall that Khadijah, the wife of Prophet Muhammad, had attained a degree of wealth and notability within the community prior to their meeting and eventual marriage, as a direct result of her business acumen in managing her caravan business. So it would seem that those who would insist on implementing purdah today, which requires women to live separated from all male non-family members, might find the statements and admonitions of the Quran non-supportive.

E. Is it true that all Muslim women must wear a veil?

The veil. Other than the cross of Jesus Christ, perhaps no other symbol has become so recognized and identifiable with a world-wide religion. The contemporary image of the women of Islam is constantly portrayed in most of the Western media as that of a barely recognizable human form, covered from the crown of the head to the soles of the feet in a morbid swath of black. But as with all other popular stereotypes, this image is not a true representation of the teaching and practice of Islam throughout the world. Once again, this author has lived, studied and lectured in numerous Islamic countries, most of which do not practice purdah or the wearing of the veil.

The history of the veil must be examined in order to gain an understanding as to why there is no unanimity among Muslim societies regarding the wearing of the veil. Veiling and seclusion (purdah) are often considered together, and wherever one is practiced the other is likely to be practiced as well. Both practices were customs assimilated from the conquered Persian and Byzantine societies. The Quran only speaks of modesty, for both men and women.

"Say to the believing men that they should lower their gaze and guard their modesty; that will make for greater purity for them; and Allah is well acquainted with all that they do. And say to the believing women that they should lower their gaze and guard their modesty; that they should not display their beauty and ornaments except what must ordinarily appear;

they should draw their veils over their bosoms and not display their beauty except to their husbands and their fathers." (Surah 24:30,31)

The rule of modesty applies to men as well as women. An obvious, public stare by a man at a woman or even another man is considered a breach of refined manners. Notice that nowhere in the text is there a command or suggestion that the woman must cover her face with a veil. The intent is to promote modesty, both internally and externally. All believers have a responsibility to conduct themselves in a morally upright manner, taking the necessary precautions to avoid causing another Muslim to spiritually or morally "stumble." This admonition is quite similar to that found in the New Testament by Paul the Apostle when writing to the Corinthian Christians where he points out the responsibility of every Christian believer towards others.

"Do not cause anyone to stumble, whether Jews, Greeks, or the church of God." (I Corinthians 10:32)

THE VEILING OF WOMEN IS FOUND IN THE BIBLE! It is surprising that most Christians are unaware that the wearing of veils was a quite common practice centuries before the birth of Islam. Consider the encounter between Isaac and Rebekah recorded in Genesis 24:62-65:

"Now Isaac had come from Beer Lahai Roi, for he was living in the Negev. He went out to the field one evening to meditate, and as he looked up, he saw camels approaching. Rebekah also looked up and saw Isaac. She got down from her camel and asked the servant 'Who is that man in the field coming to meet us?' 'He is my master,' the servant answered. So she took her veil and covered herself."

Notice the similarities between the texts of the Quran and the Bible; both suggest the veil or hijab was "drawn across or over the body" as an act of modesty. Christian believers must, like their Muslim counterparts, consciously strive to demonstrate a modicum of modesty which includes the selection of clothing worn in public.

"I also want women to dress modestly, with decency and propriety, not with braided hair or gold or pearls or expensive clothes, but with good deeds, appropriate for women who profess to worship God." (I Timothy 2:9, 10)

"Veiling" is barely mentioned in the Quran, yet the wearing of a ghata or scarf which exposes only the face has become something similar to a status symbol for many of the wealthy and educated women of Islam. The West has become aware of this symbol by observing various Muslim women of high political office who wear the ghata, such as the former Prime Minister Benazir Bhutto of Pakistan. It is not uncommon to see Muslim women wearing the ghata in many American cities while on their way to work or in the public domain.

The wearing of black dresses and veils by some women can be traced directly to opposition to the Shah of Iran in the 1970's which led to the Iranian Revolution. The people of Iran grew tired of the attempted westernization of their country and culture. As the anti-government movement grew, the women of Iran began wearing the chador, a black dress or garment which covered them from head to foot. This became the symbol of opposition to the Shah and provided the protesting women anonymity during public demonstrations. In 1979 these same women demonstrated against the establishment of a new law which would have made the chador compulsory. Although this law was rescinded, veiling was made compulsory in all government and public offices in the summer of 1980. At the same time co-education was banned, and women were barred from the judiciary and the legal profession. It is these particular events which occurred in Iran that have most influenced the perception of Islam in the west.

CONCLUSION: The Quran contains no explicit command for women to wear a veil covering their faces, nor does it command women to wear the chador. The Quran speaks of modesty, and the protection of women in public from the stares and ogling of carnal minded men by covering the most revealing parts of the female anatomy. The term "veil" as used in the Quran and the Bible is interchangeable with cloak and shaw. Rebekah used her shaw or cloak to cover her figure and become presentable before Isaac. Therefore, the emphasis of the Quran is upon modest behavior and appearance in public, and not upon the covering of the face. The idea or teaching that a woman must be completely covered in public was borne out of interpretations of the Quran, such as the exegesis of Surah 24:31 by a 13th-century Persian Muslim named al-Baydawi who was one of the more renowned Quranic scholars. Please take a moment to compare this text quoted earlier with his personal interpretation below.

> "Indeed the whole of the body is to be regarded as pudental and no part of her may lawfully be seen by anyone but her husband or close kin..."

Today, there are many Muslim women who choose to wear the hijab, the chador, or the ghata even though there is no compulsory law or societal pressure to do so. Why are they doing it? For some it is a matter of witnessing that they are Muslima, attempting to follow the tenets of Islam. But for others, it may well be an expression of disagreement and dissatisfaction with a decadent and immoral Western society which, while claiming to champion the "liberation" of women, continues to promote them as objects of sexual exploitation and amusement for the benefit of a male-dominated culture. Both Muslim men and women, liberal and conservative, are appalled and disgusted by the "modern and liberated" women's open display of themselves and the sexual freedoms viewed as part of the general emancipation of women in the West. It is best stated by Fatima Mernissi, a Muslim writer who said:

> "While it is true that some Muslim exploitation of the female is clad under veils and buried behind walls, Western exploitation has the bad taste of being unclad, bare and overexposed."

F. Does the Quran teach a "Jihad" or holy war against the west and all non-Muslims?

Along with the veil, the term "Jihad" appears regularly in the Western press and electronic media, conjuring up the image of hordes of sword-waving, wide-eyed, black-bearded Muslim men breathing death and destruction to all who resist the message of Islam and the Messenger. The term "Jihad" is bandied about as a buzz word by politicians, commentators, various religious "leaders" as well as secular humanists and atheists. Collectively, they all use the term to further their own specific agendas, and to reinforce the aspect of fear and suspicion in the minds and hearts of a largely uninformed and disinterested general population. But as with all aspects of Islam, we must seek the true meaning of Jihad from the only trustworthy source, the Holy Quran.

> "Those who believe, and suffer exile and strive with might and main, in Allah's cause, with their goods and their persons,

have the highest rank in the sight of Allah; they are the people who will achieve salvation." (Surah 9:20)

In this verse we discover the essential meaning of the Arabic word Jihad, for it is this word which appears in the text of the Quran and is rendered "strive" in the English. Jihad comes from the root J-H-D which means to strive and struggle. The usage in the Quran generally refers to any spiritual, psychological or physical effort made by a Muslim to be close to God by making the message of the Quran supreme in his or her life, and as a by-product, achieve a just and harmonious society. Jihad is short for "Jihad fi Sabeel Allah," which means "struggle in God's cause." Any Muslim who attempts to live his life as a true Muslim is considered a "Mujahid" meaning one who strives for God and justice. If a man is not willing to strive he will gain nothing, as represented in Surah 53:39 which states: "Man can have nothing but what he strives for." A Muslim tries to live his life according to the guidance given by God and His Prophet.

He also tries to promote and establish the message of Islam in society through his personal words and actions. The striving, struggle, or Jihad, is to maintain one's life on the noble pathway of God. Jihad is described in the Sunnah as a natural corollary of the five pillars of faith. Commitment to God involves commitment to sacrifice one's time, energy and wealth in order to promote the cause of truth and justice. Such commitment may even require the giving of one's life in order to preserve Truth. Jihad implies a readiness to give whatever one has, including his life, for the sake of Allah.

Perhaps the Muslim writer Al-Ghazali has captured the essence of Jihad when he said:

"The real Jihad is the warfare against the passions."

The larger and more prevalent meaning of Jihad is the spiritual struggle of the soul. The objective of Islam is to abolish the lordship of man over man, and to bring all under the rule of the One God. Jihad, then, is the attitude and willingness to stake everything you have, including your lifestyle and your very life, to achieve this goal. The struggle to gain control over one's fleshly nature and desires, and to replace those desires with the higher and more noble spiritual desires, is common to the true Christian believer as well. Consider the teaching of Jesus Christ who, when addressing His disciples concerning the high cost of following His teachings and example, warned that they all must willingly exchange their physical goals, wants, and desires for eternal ones. Such a dramatic change can only be accomplished through discipline and self denial.

> *"Then Jesus said to his disciples,'If anyone would come after me, he must deny himself and take up his cross and follow me. For whoever wants to save his life will lose it, but whoever loses his life for me will find it. What good will it be for a man if he gains the whole world, yet forfeits his soul? Or what can a man give in exchange for his soul.'" (Matthew 16:24-26)*

The Christian, like the Muslim, is expected to make his own Jihad, to so live his life that his society and environment are affected to the point of change. Paul the Apostle repeated the theme of Jesus in calling for Christians to symbolically execute their physical and carnal desires.

> *"Those who belong to Christ Jesus have crucified the sinful nature with its passions and desires. Since we live by the Spirit, let us keep in step with the Spirit." (Galatians 5:24,25)*

The popularly accepted notion that Islamic countries today are intolerant towards other religions even to the point of persecution and imprisonment, and are forcing their citizens to become Muslims, all as part of their Jihad, is simply not true. While it is true that in a very small minority of Muslim countries there is some verified harassment of Christians and in some cases, prohibition against proselytization, these countries are the exception and most certainly not the norm or rule.

> *"If it had been the Lord's will, they would all have believed... all who are on the earth. Will you then compel mankind against their will, to believe? No, let their be no compulsion in religion."(Surah 10:99)*

PAKISTAN is perhaps a good example of a Muslim nation which exercises and protects the right of freedom of religion for all its citizens. Pakistan is the second largest Muslim country in the world after Indonesia. This author has travelled to Pakistan many times concerning the plight of the people of Kahsmir and human rights. I have met and worked with the citizens of Pakistan on every level of society, from the President to educators, writers, and the common hard working citizen. Never have I, as a Christian, received even a suggestion of prejudice or disdain towards myself or my faith.

The Islamic scholar Yusuf Ali states:

> *"Compulsion is incompatible with religion because religion depends on faith and free will, and these would be meaningless if induced by force."*

It is unfortunate that Islam has been stereotyped as the "religion of the sword." As we discovered in Chapter II, early

Islam was spread by persuasion, not by military power. In those cases where any force was used, including any Muslim leaders or countries today, such forced conversion squarely contradicts the very heart of Islam which rests upon a voluntary response to the message of God.

Followers of Islam, as indeed the followers of true Christianity, Judaism, or any other world religion, are totally without justification for any use of force or compulsion in promulgating their religious beliefs.

> *"Let there be no compulsion in religion: Truth stands out clear from error; whoever rejects Evil and believes in Allah has grasped the most trustworthy handhold, that never breaks."* (Surah 2:256)

> *"Invite all to the way of your Lord with wisdom and beautiful preaching; and argue with them in ways that are best and most gracious: For your Lord knows best who strayed from His Path and who receive guidance."* (Surah 16:125)

The term "Holy War" so popularized in the Western media deserves a closer examination. It is this term or phrase which is constantly quoted and referenced by those whose personal or political agendas include the demonization of Islam. As with all of the distortions and misconceptions concerning the true teachings and tenets of Islam, the "Holy War" must be examined and understood within the boundary of historical context.

> *"Fight for the sake of Allah those that fight against you, but do not attack them first. Allah does not love aggressors."* (Surah 2:190)

From its very beginning, Islam, like Christianity, was a new and hated religion by those citizens of Arabia who had long worshipped numerous idols, materialism, and assorted deities. As Muhammad and the first believers of Islam tried to proclaim their faith they were met with ridicule, mockery, and eventually, violent physical attacks. These early Muslims were cut off from the society of Mecca, unable to preach their faith in public, forbidden to buy or sell in the markets, or to marry outside of their faith. This "boycott" was eventually lifted by the non-Muslims as it lost its effectiveness. But persecution continued, until a secret meeting of the leaders of the dominant tribes was held and it was agreed that each tribe would select an assassin who would collectively murder Muhammad while asleep in his bed.

Islamic history records the story of how God instructed Muhammad to leave the city of Mecca and go to Medina to join with other Muslims who had already fled the persecution. This event became known as the Great Event or Hijrah which means Emigration, and it is this event which marks the beginning of Islamic history and the Islamic Calendar.

Physical attacks continued to escalate, and eventually the Muslims were forced to defend themselves by forming an army. Having become the oppressed and not the oppressor, God gave a new revelation to the faithful:

> "Verily God will defend those who believe: God loves not any that is a traitor to faith or shows ingratitude. To those against whom war is made, permission is given to fight, because they are wronged; and verily, God is Most Powerful for their aid; those who have been expelled from their homes in defiance of right, (for no cause) except they say: 'Our Lord is God.' Did not God check one set of people by means of another, there would surely have been pulled down monasteries, churches, syna-

gogues, and mosques, in which the name of God is commemo-
rated in abundant measure. God will certainly aid those who
aid His (cause); for verily God is Full of strength, Exalted in
Might, (Able to enforce His Will)." (Surah 22:39, 40)

I hope that the reader will finally understand that this final phase or level of "Jihad" popularly known as a "Holy War" began as a direct result of the persecution of Muslims, and that the key Quranic passages clearly indicate that warfare was, and is, to be purely defensive in nature. If indeed Muslim political leaders, governments, or regimes are waging wars of aggression anywhere, they do so without the support of the Quran or the example of Prophet Muhammad.

Christians and Christianity have long held the belief that they (and therefore, Christianity) are justified in participating in warfare as long as it can be considered valid in light of the "just war theory." Likewise, Islam contains very specific rules and criteria in order for a true Jihad to be declared. A Muslim may engage in an act of Jihad of the sword only when defending himself, his family or country, his faith, and in the defense of his fellow Muslims who are truly helpless and oppressed.

CONCLUSION: History reveals that all of the major religions engaged in "Holy Wars" against their fellow human beings. After all, a mere ten generations have passed since Christian armies, operating within a clear tradition and inspired by a coherent ideology, were winning the land war against the Turks in the Balkans. Today's modern Christian "sacred violence" is usually restricted to churches in poor countries, although one can trace the tragic civil war in Lebanon to the lingering, romanticized memory of a "golden age" under crusader rule by the Lebanese Maronites, whose church submitted to Rome in the year 1180.

Likewise, the Croats and Serbs seem to have romanticized the disasters and triumphs of the Balkan wars against the Turks. The recent human tragedy in the former Yugoslavia, in which primarily Muslims were targeted for genocide under the guise of "ethnic cleansing," can perhaps be linked to the Christian's own version of "Jihad" in imitation of their crusading forefathers.

Both Christians and Muslims are under the authority of God and both are prohibited from waging war against the innocent civilian populations of the world. Both are permitted to defend themselves and their loved ones, as well as the helpless and the truly oppressed. Sadly, both have been guilty of allowing for the politicization of their religions both in the past and the present. It is the hope of this author that this book will serve the dual purpose of the illumination of historical truths thereby leading to mutual tolerance and respect between Islam and Christianity, and the prevention of the "new Crusader wars" if the renewed Muslim aggressiveness of the 1990's should meet a revival of Christian theories of positive force.

Chapter Six
Islam and Christianity: Coalition or Collision?

A. Contemporary Islam: At the writing of this book, Islam continues to be the fastest growing religion in the world, as nearly two billion of the world's six billion population practice the tenets of Islam. The coming new century promises to present a new and altered world-view, far different from the one most familiar to the current inhabitants. As Islam continues its "re-emergence" as one of the world's largest faiths, political and economic realities will undergo dramatic change; old alliances will be replaced by new ones, and old borders established by blood and steel will become obsolete. In this the sixth and final chapter, we will continue to answer the most commonly asked questions concerning contemporary Islam, as well as exploring the possibilities of Christians and Muslims working together for the cause of Peace.

"AREN'T ALL ARABS MUSLIMS, AND ALL MUSLIMS ARABS?"

Another very popular Western stereotype of Islam. The origin of this assumption can perhaps be traced to the early historical textbooks published in the western nations which stressed the origination of Islam by, with, and among the inhabitants of Arabia. Also, since the Quran was written in Arabic, and Muslim believers must learn to speak and read Arabic, it seemed a logical conclusion that Islam is indeed an "Arabic religion" which is patently false.

It is usually a shock to those living in the west to learn that the countries with the largest populations of Muslims are not Arabic at all, but rather are to be found in Asia. Here are a few examples:

Indonesia ....185 million
Pakistan ....120 million
Bangladesh ....113 million
Iran ....60 million

Even those countries which are not Islamic have more Muslim citizens then the Arab nations, such as:

India ....140 million
China ....100 million
USSR (former) ....70 million

It is important to note that these figures are constantly changing as the populations of these countries continue to increase, and the breakup of the former Soviet Union continues and religious freedom is once again available.

In the West, the number of Muslims is likewise very difficult to trace due to the constant increase in immigration and other factors. It is a fact that France, Germany, and Great Britain are quite concerned with the explosion of Muslim immigrants into their countries over the past decade and have passed restrictive immigration laws in an effort to stop what the western press has continually labeled "the Islamic invasion."

It is believed there are more than eight million Muslims in America and growing. Islam, as of 1997, had become the second largest religion in America. Although the Muslim community is generally quiet and low-key, it has already demonstrated its collective influence on national and local politics, adopting the "American Way" of lobbying, fund-raising for friendly candidates, and all-out opposition against political enemies. One striking example of their political expertise is revealed in the ending of the long standing Pressler Amendment which restricted military sales to

Pakistan. U.S. Congressmen, Senators, even the President and Vice President, are sensitive and responsive to the issues deemed important to the American Muslim community. For American Muslims, the highlight of the year 1996 was the program held in the White House and hosted by Hilary Clinton, wife of President Bill Clinton, celebrating Eid Mubarak, the end of the of Holy month of Ramadan. This was the first Eid celebration ever held in the White House, and most assuredly reflects the impact Islam continues to have upon America, its citizens, and government leaders.

As Muslim populations continue to increase, the face of Europe and the West is changing, as mosques and Islamic Centers, women wearing the Hijab (head scarf), and Islamic schools and universities are becoming more common place and integrated within the culture and customs of the West. The United States government has commissioned the first military chaplains for their armed forces as well as the federal prison systems. Many states have followed by recruiting Muslim chaplains for their penal systems. The Quran is now included in various public chapels such as those found in the largest airports and train stations. Muslim chaplains are now on call and available at many major hospitals and care facilities throughout America.

B. CONTRIBUTIONS OF ISLAM BENEFIT ALL MANKIND

Europcentricity: the view that all discoveries, inventions, and innovations contributing to the betterment of mankind can all be traced to a predominantly white European culture. "Civilization" and sophistication it is said, are the exclusive "side benefits" of the Age of Reason and the Renaissance. Such historical arrogance and deception is clearly evident in such famous books of history as History Generale by Alfred Ramfield published in 1892. Of the 291 chapters of "world" history, a full 250 are about Europe.

It is important to note that while Europe languished in what is known as "the dark ages" which include the 7th through the 13th centuries, the Islamic world advanced intellect and culture to such an advanced state that this same period became known as "The Golden Age of Islam." For a more in-depth study of the contribution of Islam to the world community, I refer the reader once again to the Suggested Reading List at the close of the book. Here are a few of the more prominent contributions:

1. ART... The prohibition against depicting human forms which might become the object of worship or veneration is found in both the Bible and the saying of the Prophet in the Hadith. This in turn encouraged the creation of abstract art which crystallized into three basic forms:

A. Geometrical... with intricate geometric shapes with overlaying squares, rectangles, triangles, etc. This art form is seen in much of today's "modern" art.

B. Arabesque... Reflecting the unity of creation and God, Arabesque art is comprised of interconnecting lines, interlacing rosettes, intertwining vines and interweaving curves, reflecting growth, change and movement.

C. Calligraphic... Islam, like Christianity, is totally united with its religious guide book, the Quran. Devout Muslim calligraphers attempted to make the Quran more appealing to the eye. Calligraphy and Recitation of the Quran became the vocations held in the highest esteem in Islam.

2. ARCHITECTURE... Millions of world travellers have been awed by their first viewing of the Taj Mahal in Agra, India, the Blue Mosque in Istanbul, Turkey, Masjid-Shah in Isfahan, Iran, or the Badshahi Mosque in Lahore, Pakistan. As a tribute to Islamic architects, mosques have been called "calligraphy in architectural form" and "theology in concrete." Islamic architecture has been adopted around the

world, especially in Europe and North America, and can be seen in what is considered the most exquisite of American private homes, office buildings, shopping malls, even the U.S. Capitol in Washington, D.C.

3. SCIENCE... The Golden Age of Islam produced so many of the world's geniuses in a variety of fields including Mathematics, Physics, and Medicine, that it was also known as the "Classical Period." By the 8th century, Baghdad was the unchallenged intellectual center of the world. "The House of Wisdom", founded by Caliph Mamun who ruled Baghdad from 813-833, trained Muslim scientists and scholars from whom the Europeans gleaned their knowledge of ancient classical greek thought and philosophy. The European Renaissance is heavily indebted to the contributions of Muslim scholars as evidenced by the famous painting by Raphael entitled "The School of Athens" in which he included the Muslims.

4. PHYSICS... Muslims were the first to invent the clock pendulum, the magnetic compass, and the astrolabe. They created precision instruments to measure special weights and gravities of elements. Ibn al Haytham (1039) was the founder of optics through his studies on the reflection and refraction of light.

5. MATHEMATICS... Algebra, an Arabic word meaning "to restore broken parts" was invented by the Persian scientist Muhammad ibn Musa al-Khwarizmi in the year 850. Borrowing the zero from India, he later established a system of counting which today is known as Arabic numerals. Muslim scholars also developed plane geometry and trigonometry which the west adopted as "their own."

6. MEDICINE... The first hospital as we know it today was built in Baghdad in the year 706. By the tenth century, a fully staffed medical school and hospital featuring outpatient

clinics, pharmacies and libraries was operational in Baghdad. Muslim doctors were the first to:

a. use anesthesia during surgery.

b. cauterize wounds.

c. discover epidemics arise from contagion through touch and air.

d. create an ambulatory hospital transported on the back of a camel.

e. separate pharmacology from medicine and the writing of prescriptions.

By the tenth-century, Muslim doctors were setting bones, performing cancer surgery, removing cataracts, and performing skull surgery. By the year 925 Abu Bakr Muhammad al-Razi was experimenting with music therapy, how to differentiate between smallpox and measles, and the study of pediatrics.

CONCLUSION: Neither space nor time permit the further enumeration of contributions made as a result of Islam and its adherents. Other important contributions can be found in Literature, Astronomy, Prose and Poetry, and Philosophy.

D. CHRISTIANS AND MUSLIMS FOR PEACE

CAMP began as a dream in my heart in 1970 while I was studying archaeology in that ancient land called Palestine. I was in daily contact with the Palestinians whom we paid as workers for our excavation projects. Along with all the other American, Canadian, and British students, I was very surprised to learn of the deep and abiding faith of the Palestinian Arabs who called themselves Muslims.

Each and every day, as we toiled together in the relentless heat and the summer sun, excavating the remains of bygone emperor's and dynasties, these Muslim men would pause, face Mecca, and pray to God as the call to prayer echoed from hundreds of minarets across Jerusalem, and indeed, across Palestine, the middle east, and around the world. Responding to the genuine warmth and hospitality of the Palestinian People, I soon was invited not only to their homes to share their wonderful food and culture, but also to attend the Maghrib (after sunset) prayers at the Dome of the Rock and the Al-Aqsa Mosque.

It was then that I began to read and study the Quran and Islam for myself, and I soon discovered the tremendous amount of common ground between my Christian faith and the true faith and teachings of Islam. And it was then that I began to dream and envision the relationship of Christians and Muslims, Islam and Christianity, on a world-wide scale, not as it was, intolerant and suspicious of each other, but rather finding enough in common to permit them to live and work together in peace.

In 1987 I was a guest in the home of the Grand Mufti of Syria, His Excellency Sheikh Ahmad Kuftaro. My wife and I spent several hours discussing Islam and Christianity. After examining our differences, we began to focus on our common ground, and our discussion lasted for hours. Upon leaving his residence, the Grand Mufti remarked "we have so much in common, we are in the same camp." Later, while flying on an airplane to Lebanon, I wrote the word camp, and then the acronym, CHRISTIANS AND MUSLIMS FOR PEACE!

It is important for the reader to clearly understand what CAMP IS NOT, as well as what it is. CAMP is not an inter-faith organization, attempting to bring Christians, Jews, and Muslims together. There are numerous such groups and organizations throughout the world. Neither is CAMP a Christian or Church missionary project or outreach in an effort or attempt to convert Muslims to Christianity. CAMP is not a movement to form Islam and Christianity into one religion. CAMP is not financed by or a part of any political party or government.

CAMP is an organization of Christian and Muslim people, citizens of the world, who, because of the common ground which so clearly exists between their respective religions, believe that by working together within their communities, villages and nations, current wars and conflicts in which Christians and Muslims oppose one another can be brought to an end, and future wars and conflicts can be avoided.

CAMP membership is open to any and all Christians and Muslims who long to see a world free of war and suffering; who truly believe that God commands those who truly worship Him to be peacemakers; men and women who are willing to extend the hand of friendship to their fellow man, eschewing the hate and prejudices of political policies and cultural prejudices.

E. The urgent need for meaningful dialogue

As this book goes to press in the year 1998, Christians and Muslims continue to engage in brutal wars and civil conflicts in Africa, Asia, Europe and the Middle East. In Sudan, Christians in the South accuse the northern government of attempted genocide, sending its army to attack unarmed civilians in remote villages, kidnapping women and children to be sold or used in slavery. The Northern Islamic government of Khartoum accuses the Christians armies, especially one calling itself "the Lord's Army,"of targeting civilian populations, forcibly conscripting boys as young as eight and ten years of age into their "volunteer" ranks.

In Azerbaijan, the Muslim government continues its nine year warfare against the Christian Armenian forces now occupying the war zone known as Nagorno Karabakh. Millions of Muslim civilians have been driven from their homes, separated from their families, cut off from the land and the homes they have lived in for centuries.

Throughout Asia, civil strife continues between Christians and Muslims as churches and mosques are burned and desecrated, Imams and Pastors are beaten and killed, and entire villages attack other villages, often shooting, hacking, and in many cases stomping and burning to death their "religious enemies." Rape of the young and the old is a common strategy employed by both sides.

In Bosnia, Christians and Muslims re-arm themselves for what both consider will be a resumption of the bloody war within the former Soviet satellite country of Yugoslavia, once the United Nations and United States forces withdraw from the region.

In the Western European states, Christian and Muslim citizens exchange bitter rhetoric and accusations; public demonstrations and marches against immigrant Muslims is common. Homes and housing projects are firebombed, as hate and intolerance increase. In the United States, accusations of "terrorism" appear daily in both the print and electronic media. Fear, distrust, and suspicion continue to alienate American citizens in the same cities, schools and workplace.

WHAT IS THE ANSWER? WHAT CAN BE DONE? In those countries where actual warfare is ongoing between those claiming to be Christians and Muslims, both the leadership and the citizens must be confronted with the COMMON GROUND that both great religions share, some of which has been presented in this book. Politicians and army generals must face the fact that neither the Bible nor the Quran condone aggressive wars; that rape and torture are utterly condemned and reprehensible; and the taking of any human being anywhere in the world for the purpose of slavery is totally unjustifiable in the twenty-first century.

No true believer and self-proclaimed "servant of God," whether Army Generals, Presidents or Prime Ministers, Pastors or Imams, rich or poor, ignorant or educated, none can claim that God supports and approves of their barbarity and inhumanity against their fellow man.

F. CAMP PROGRAMS AND PROJECTS PROVIDE AN ANSWER!

The only hope to resolve and end the wars and acts of hatred and intolerance between Muslims and Christians is to seek and promote dialogue, and this is precisely the purpose and function of CAMP. Through the establishing of CAMP Chapters, Christians and Muslims meet together to discuss the greatest needs of their villages, cities, and nations. Working together, these two great religions carry out the primary command of both faiths, to take care of the poor, the homeless, the helpless and the innocent, and to demonstrate Mercy, Compassion, and Tolerance in political policies and everyday living.

Through CAMP Chapters, the truly poor and hungry are being fed and clothed; the orphans and the widows are being cared for by the community. Christian and Muslim women alternate weekly gatherings in each other's homes, cooking and preparing food for the hungry; mosques and churches work together to promote used clothing drives; Christian and Muslim men gather at the CAMP office or center to discuss how together, they can help to rebuild the homes of their neighbors destroyed by war or natural phenomena.

Through CAMP, Muslim and Christian politicians and military generals can meet face to face to explore the possibilities of ending their conflicts, knowing that CAMP is totally neutral and unbiased, seeking only to promote Peace, Justice, and Reconciliation.

CAMP sponsors one week retreats for Christian and Muslim youths, during which time they examine the common ground between their religions, and focus on how they can and must learn to end old hatreds and prejudices in order to live in harmony, peace, and mutual respect with their fellow Christian or Muslim neighbors.

A FINAL WORD

Dear reader, whether you are a Muslim or a Christian, the final question I must ask is this: what will you do with the knowledge and information you have gained from reading this book? Will you simply treat that knowledge as purely intellectual information from just another book and continue to live your life still embracing the distortions and misrepresentations, the stereotypes and prejudices, of so many past generations? Will you choose to remain in the "comfort zone" of religious arrogance and imagined superiority, "bashing and trashing" the other religion and its sincere followers and believers? Will you remain silent in the company of your fellow believers even though you have personally formed a new and more charitable attitude towards Islam or Christianity as a result of reading this book?

Or will you give thanks to God for the new insight and perspective you have gained from reading this book? Will you determine to do more research and reading about these two great religions of the world, and pledge to tell others of the truths you have discovered? Perhaps you will be the first to propose a CAMP seminar in your city, town, or village, in the hope of establishing a CAMP chapter which will serve the interests of the whole community.

I am encouraged by what some Christians and Muslims have already accomplished throughout the world by working together, as in Pakistan, where Muslim and Christian volunteers administer a leprosarium; in Indonesia, where

Muslim and Christian women banded together to oppose the slavery of lower class women such as the poor and the prostitutes; in Denmark, where Muslims and Christians run a shelter for battered women; in the Philippines, where Muslims and Christians have formed organizations to care for the aged and infirm, and provide schools and medical clinics for the poorest of the poor.

I am encouraged that in Libya, Christian women are welcome and work with the local health personnel and services to help care for the sick; even in Jerusalem where Muslims and Christians formed the "Justice and Peace" Commission which has made strong statements against oppression of the Palestinian People, and consistently making proposals for a just and lasting peace; in Upper Egypt where a team of Christians and Muslims visits numerous villages teaching and encouraging the need for family planning.

I am encouraged by the true Muslim believers who have assisted Christian drought victims in Capo Verde; and true Christian believers whose relief organizations continue to work together with local Muslim groups in Ethiopia and Pakistan. I am encouraged when a bishop in Lebanon reported that his cathedral was destroyed by Muslim extremists but was immediately rebuilt by local Muslim merchants.

I am encouraged that in Libya, when word spread that a priest and a group of Christians were seeking a place to hold a communion service, the Muslims of the town offered the use of their local mosque and the service was held.

CHRISTIANS AND MUSLIMS ARE WORKING TOGETHER THROUGHOUT THE WORLD! Now is the time to build on the foundations of existing coalitions and cooperation; now is the time to teach all Muslims and all Christians everywhere about the COMMON GROUND they share:

(1) Common Origin... both religions find their roots in biblical Judaism, thus both place great importance on the Torah or Pentateuch (first five books of the Bible).

(2) Common Patriarch... both religions consider themselves "sons and daughters of Abraham."

(3) Common God... both are monotheistic religions and both ascribe similar attributes to the One and Only God including Creator, Sustainor, Ultimate Judge, Merciful and Compassionate; The One and Only God willing to intervene in man's history for the ideals of peace, justice, and harmony.

(4) Common Theological Beliefs such as a Divine command to spread their faith to the entire world; that man must learn to live on a higher moral and ethical plane; that repentance for willful disobedience to divine instruction is necessary for eternal life; that believers must seek the Will of God in all avenues of life, with the Muslim it is "Insh'Allah" and the Christian "The Lord's Will."

(5) Common Belief in the Virgin Birth of Jesus and high esteem for Mary (Maryam).

(6) Common Eschatology... for both believe that the world and human life will end with the consummation of the ages, the destruction of the world in a cataclysmic, chaotic fireball; both believe that Jesus Christ will return in what both call "the last day."

(7) Common Belief in a Last Judgment... when all who have lived will stand in judgment to answer for their deeds.

(8) Common Belief in the Resurrection from the dead.

(9) Common Belief in an Eternal After Life in Heaven or Paradise (Garden to the Muslim) or Hell (Fire).

(10) Common Call for Believers to make their faith a living faith by uniting faith and life, prayer and action. Christians and Muslims must actively care for Truth, stand for the

innocent, the helpless and the oppressed, while opposing the aggressor, evil, and injustice.

> *(This will be) their cry therein; "Glory to Thee, O Allah!" And "Peace" will be their greeting therein! And the close of their cry Will be: "Praise be to Allah, the Cherisher and Sustainer Of the Worlds!" (Surah 10:10)*

> *"Except those who repent and believe, and work righteousness: for these will enter the Garden and will not be wronged in the least... Gardens of Eternity, those which Allah, Most Gracious, has promised to His servants in the unseen: for His promise must come to pass. They will not there hear any vain discourse, but only salutations of Peace: and they will have therein their sustenance, morning and evening. (Surah 19:60-62)*

> *"And into whatever city or village you enter, inquire who is worthy in it; and abide there until you go away. And as you enter the house, give it your greeting. And if the house is worthy, let your greeting of peace come upon it." (Matthew 10:11-13)*

> *"But the wisdom that comes from heaven is first of all pure; then peace-loving, considerate, submissive, full of mercy and good fruit, impartial and sincere. Peacemakers who sow in peace raise a harvest of righteousness." (James 3:17)*

> *"Blessed are the peacemakers, for they shall be called sons of God." (Matthew 5:9)*

Glossary of Arabic Terms

Ablution	Ritual washing before praying.
Abu Bakr	First Caliph in Medina.
Adhan	Muslim call to prayer.
Ahl al-kitab	"People of the Book" refers to Jews and Christians, followers of the Bible.
Ali	Son-in-law of Prophet Muhammad who married the Prophet's daughter Fatima; first Imam of the Shi'ites.
Allah	The One and Only God; One to be worshipped.
Allahu Akbar	"God is Great" or "Greater is God."
Asr	The third prayer; the afternoon prayer.
Aya	A verse of the Quran.
Ayatollah	Shi'ite religious leader of high authority.
Bismalah	Islamic invocation of God: "In the name of the merciful Lord of mercy," which prefaces every Surah of the Quran except Surah 9.
Caliph	Successor to Muhammad; one who rules a Muslim nation.
Dawah	"Call"; missionary effort to spread Islam.
Dhimmi	Non-Muslims living as protected minorities in an Islamic state. (people of the book).
Din	Religion in general; religious duties in particular.

Dua	Spontaneous prayer as opposed to Salat or prescribed prayer.
Fatwah	Legal opinion given by religious leader.
Fatima	Daughter of Muhammad, wife of Ali.
Gabriel	Angel God used to reveal Quran to Muhammad.
Hadith	"Tradition", reports of the sayings or the actions of Muhammad; second in authority to the Quran.
Hafiz	One who memorizes the entire Quran.
Hajj	Fifth Pillar of Islam; pilgrimage to Mecca.
Hanif	One who knew and practiced Islam before the Quran was received; Abraham and others.
Halas	Anything approved by the sacred law of God.
Haram	Anything forbidden by the sacred law of God.
Hasan	Son of Ali; grandson of Prophet Muhammad and second Imam of the Shi'ites.
Hijra	Emigration of Muhammad from Mecca to Medina in 622; first year of Islamic lunar calendar.
Hira	Cave Outside Mecca where Muhammad received the first revelation of the Quran from Gabriel.
Hezbollah	Party of God.

Iblis	Satan
Imam	General term for leader of prayer; for the Shiite he is a spiritual guide.
Iman	"Faith"
Injil	"Gospel"; revelation given to Jesus.
Insha 'Allah	God willing. "If Allah wills".
Islam	Submission to Allah; religion of Quran.
Jihad	Striving for a moral, spiritual or political goal because of Islam; one who struggles is called a Mujtahid.
Jinn	Invisible spiritual creatures in the Quran.
Kabah	"Cube"; cube-shaped building in Mecca; the "Holy of Holies" for pilgrims and the place toward which all Muslims face to pray.
Khadijah	First wife of Prophet Muhammad.
Khatib	Preacher of mosque, delivers Friday sermon.
Khutba	Sermon given at Friday noon prayer.
Mahdi	"The guided one"; a messianic figure many believe will come to promote righteousness before the world ends; called "al-Mahdi."
Masjid	Mosque; literally, a place of prostration.
Mecca	Location of Kabah; birthplace of Muhammad; Muslims perform Hajj or pilgrimage to Mecca.

Mihrab	Arched niche in the wall of every mosque which is the Qibla or direction of Mecca.
Minbar	Pulpit from which sermons are preached at the Friday noon prayers.
Muazzin	One who calls the Faithful to prayer.
Mufti	Qualified Islamic religious leader.
Mujaddid	The renewer, restorer, or reformer in Islam; One is to come in every century.
Mujahidun	Soldiers of Allah.
Nabi	A prophet.
Qibla	Direction of the Kabah; direction of prayer.
Quran	"Recitation"; Islam's Scripture given by God to Muhammad by angel Gabriel.
Ramadan	The month of fasting for all Muslims.
Salam	"Peace"; a greeting, salutation, blessing.
Salat	Ritual prayer; one of five pillars of faith; performed five times a day.
Sawm	Fasting, during Ramadan; a pillar of faith.
Shahada	"Witness"; first pillar of Islam:"There is no God but God and Muhammad is His Prophet."
Shariah	Islamic law derived from Quran and Hadith and the Sunna.
Sheikh	"Mature, full of wisdom"; title of respect.
Shiite	"Partisan"; Muslims who believe Ali was the successor to Muhammad, called Shi'ites.

Shirk	Associating anything with Allah; idolatry.
Sufi	Muslim mystic; seek direct experience with God. Sufi's called brotherhoods.
Sunna	Tradition and custom of Muhammad; like the Hadith, second in authority to the Quran.
Sunni	Largest branch of Islam; those who follow the teachings of the Prophet.
Surah	A chapter of the Quran; total of 114 surahs.
Tawhid	Doctrine of the Divine Unity of God.
Ulema	Scholars of Islamic law.
Umma	Muslim community.
Wudu	Ritual ablution or purification by washing before Salat or prayer.
Zakat	Almsgiving; one of Five Pillars of Islam.

Suggested Reading List

Ali, Abdullah Yusef. The Holy Quran, Text, Translation, and Commentary. McGregor and Werner, Inc. 1946

Arberry, Arthur J., Translator. The Koran Interpreted. New York: MacMillan Publishing Company, 1976.

Pickkthall, M. Marmaduke, Translator. The Meaning of the Glorious Koran. New York American Library, 1963.

Abdalatil, Hammudah. Islam in Focus. American Trust Publications. Indianapolis, Indiana, 1976.

Ahamd, Khurshid, ed. Islam: Its Meaning and Message. Leicester, England: The Islamic Foundation, 1980

Ahmad, Mumtaz, ed. State Politics and Islam. Indianapolis Indiana: American Trust Publications, 1986.

Al-Faruqi, Ismail. Islam. Niles, Illinois: Argus Publications, 1984.

Ali, M. Muhammad. A Manual of Hadith. Lahore, Pakistan.

Arnold, Sir T.W. The Caliphate. Oxford, U.K., 1924.

Assam, Abd-al-Rahman. The Eternal Message of Muhammad. London: Quartet Books, 1979.

Azzam, A.R.. The Eternal Message of Muhammad. Translated by Caesar E. Farah. New York, 1964.

Bell, Richard. Introduction to the Quran. Edinburgh, U.K.: Edinburgh University Press, 1963.

Berger, Morroe. The Arab World. New York: Anchor Books 1964.

Braswell, George W. Jr. ISLAM: It's Prophet, Peoples, Politics, and Power. Nashville: Broadman and Holman, 1996.

Bucaille, Maurice. The Bible, the Quran and Science. Indianapolis: North American Trust Publications, 1979.

Cragg, Kenneth. The Call of the Minaret. New York: Oxford University Press, 1964.

——————————— Muhammad and the Christian. Maryknoll: Orbis Books, 1984.

——————————— Jesus and the Muslim. London: George Allen and Unwin Ltd., 1985.

Cragg, Kenneth, and R. Marston Speight. The House of Islam. Belmont: Wadsworth Publishing Company, 1988.

——————————— Islam from Within. Belmont: Wadsworth Publishing Company, 1980.

Donohue, John J. and Esposito, John L., eds. Islam in Transition: Muslim Perspectives. New York: Oxford University Press, 1982.

Donzel, E. Van. Islamic Desk Reference. New York: E.J. Brill, 1994.

Esposito, John L. "Islamic Revivalism." The Muslim World. Occasional Paper No.3, 1985.

——————————— ,ed. Voices of Resurgent Islam. New York: Oxford Press, 1983.

Farah, Caesar E. ISLAM. New York: Barron's Educational Series, 1987 edition.

Glasse, Cyril. A Concise Encyclopedia of Islam. San Francisco: Harper and Row, 1989.

Haddad, Yvonne Y. Contemporary Islam and the Challenge of History. Edison, New Jersey: State University of New York Press, 1981.

——————————— , ed. The Muslims of America. New York: Oxford University Press, 1991.

Hamidullah, Muhammad. Introduction to Islam. Paris: Centre Cultural Islamizue, 1969.

Haykal, Muhammad Husayn. The Life of Muhammad. Indianapolis: American Trust Publications, 1976.

Kimball, Charles. Striving Together: A Way Forward In ChristianMuslim Relations. New York: Orbis Books, 1991.

Kritzeck, James. "Muslim-Christian Understandings in Medieval Times." in Comparative Studies in Society and History. Volume 4, 1962.

Lewis, Bernard. The Arabs in History. New York: Harper and Row, 1967.

——————————— Islam in History. New York: The Library Press, 1973.

Mernissi, Fatima. Beyond the Veil. New York: Halsted Press, 1975.

Mohaddessin, Mohammad. Islamic Fundamentalism. Washington: Seven Locks Press, 1993.

Muslim-Christian Research Group. The Challenge of the Scriptures: The Bible and the Quran. Maryknoll, New York: Orbis Books, 1989.

Nasr, Sayyed Hossein. Ideals and Realities of Islam. Boston: Beacon Press, 1972.

————————, ed. Islamic Spirituality. New York: Crossroad, 1987.

O'Leary, DeLacy. Arabia Before Muhammad. New York: Kegan Paul and Co., 1927.

Parrinder, Geoffrey. Jesus in the Quran. New York: Oxford Univesity Press, 1977.

Parshall, Phil. Inside the Community: Understanding Muslims Through Their Traditions. Grand Rapids: Baker Books, 1994.

Qaradawi, Yusuf. The Lawful and the Prohibited in Islam. Lahore: Islamic Publications Ltd., 1991.

Saud, Muhammad. Islam and Evolution of Science. Islamabad: Islamic Research Institute, 1988.

Schuon, Frithjof. Understanding Islam. Baltimore: Penguin Books, 1972.

Smith, William Cantwell. Islam in Modern History. Princeton: Princeton University Press, 1957.

———————— . On Understanding Islam. The Hague: Mouton Publishers, 1981.

Speight, Marston. God is One: The Way of Islam. New York: Friendship Press, 1989.

Watt, W. Montgomery. The Faith and Practice of Al-Ghazali. Chicago: Kazi Publications, 1982.

————————-. Muhammad: Prophet and Statesman. London: Oxford University Press, 1977.

Zepp, Ira G. A Muslim Primer. Westminster: Wakefield Editions, 1992.

Index

*CAMP Founder & President William Baker addressing
audience attending the first CAMP dinner held May 1, 1997*

William Baker meeting Dr. Muzammil Siddiqi,
President of the Islamic Society of North America

William Baker meeting with Imam Warith Deen Mohammed,
respected leader of more than one million African American Muslims
and Founder of the Muslim American Society.

William Baker and His Excellency Sheikh Ahmad Kuftaro,
Grand Mufti of Syria

William Baker meeting with Imams and Muslim
leaders from Pakistan, Syria, and the United States.

William Baker meeting with delegation of Ogaden Muslims from North Africa

William Baker meeting with member of Parliament in an Islamic country

William Baker meeting with members of the Organization of Islamic Countries

Meeting with Islamic leaders from the Middle East and Asia

Discussion with Islamic leaders from Morocco, Tunis, and Malaysia

Guest speaker for the annual Council of Islamic Organizations

Speaking to Islamic Conference during Ramadan

Author in midst of Kashmiri Muslims in Kashmir

Speaking at Human Rights March at Hyde Park, London England

Author with Prime Minister of Azad Kashmir

Testifying at the United Nations Human Rights Commission, Geneva

Displaying the Faisal Gold Medal Peace Award

*Conference attendees extending congratulations
on receiving the Faisal Gold Medal*

*Dr. Muzammil Siddiqi and Dr. Robert H. schuller, prominent leaders
of Islam and Christianity, meet during the CAMP dinner held on
the campus of the Crystal Cathedral during 1997*